ISLAM and International Relations

ISLAM and International Relations

Edited by

J. HARRIS PROCTOR

FREDERICK A. PRAEGER, *Publishers*
New York · Washington · London

BOOKS THAT MATTER

Published in the United States of America in 1965
by Frederick A. Praeger, Inc., Publishers
111 Fourth Avenue, New York 3, N.Y.

Library of Congress Catalog Card Number: 65-12192

Printed in the United States of America

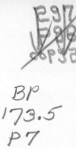

Preface

The origin of this volume is to be found in discussions that took place in 1962 among the professors of Economics, History, Languages, Law, Political Science, and Religion who constituted the Duke University Committee on International Relations. This group became intrigued by the question of how modern world politics has been affected by Islam, and decided that this was a topic that merited a more systematic and comprehensive inquiry than it had yet received. Accordingly, leading scholars from throughout the United States were invited to prepare papers dealing with various specific aspects of the general theme "Islam and International Relations," which would be presented at a conference of academic specialists on the Muslim world and then published in the form of a symposium-style book. The conference met at Duke University from June 10 to 13, 1963, and brought together faculty members from twenty-six colleges and universities for an encounter that was both interdisciplinary and intercultural. The authors were thereupon allowed to revise their papers in the light of the conference discussions.

Sir Hamilton A. R. Gibb, Director of the Center for Middle Eastern Studies at Harvard University, opens the symposium with a comparative study of attitudes toward the civil authority in Islamic and Christian countries and an inquiry into the consequences of the Muslim pattern of social integration for political action at both the national and the international level. Consideration is then given to the present-day significance of Islamic doctrines regarding international relations by Majid Khadduri, Director of the Center for Middle East Studies at the School of Advanced International Studies of The Johns Hopkins University; he describes the modifications that have been made in the classical theory and suggests ways in which Islam may contribute to the emergence of a world order. There follows an empirical analysis of the response on the part of Muslim states in the Middle East to the Soviet challenge by Dankwart A. Rustow, Professor of International Social Forces at the School of International Affairs of Columbia University and member of the Brookings Institution's Foreign Policy Studies Senior Staff, in which the limited effectiveness of Soviet policy is attributed to political rather than religious factors. Fayez Sayegh, then Barclay Acheson Professor of International Studies at Macalaster College and now Associate Professor of Political Studies at the American University of Beirut, next develops by a variety of methods the thesis that the adoption of a neutralist position in world affairs is quite unrelated to the profession of Islam.

In the second half of the symposium, emphasis shifts to the impact of Islam on the relations of Muslim states *inter se*. Bayard Dodge, President-Emeritus of the American University of Beirut, offers an historical survey of the connection between Islam and Arab nationalism and argues that this association, although threatened by secularism and the appeals of the Communist and Western alternatives, will continue to be a close one. P. J. Vatikiotis, Professor of Government and Chairman of the Committee on Near Eastern Studies at Indiana University, focuses on the use of Islam in the policy of Egypt vis-à-vis other Arab states, examining particularly how the institutions and men of religion in Cairo have supported the regime's efforts to export its socialist revolution and to lead the Arab peoples to unity. Islamic influences on the relations among the various states of Africa are explored by Vernon McKay, Director of the Program of African Studies at the School of Advanced International Studies of The Johns Hopkins University; they are found to be numerous but not clearly of primary importance. T. Cuyler Young, Chairman of the Department of Oriental Studies at Princeton University, brings the volume to a close with a study of Pan-Islamism; he stresses that its contemporary champions are concerned principally with the religious and cultural dimensions of the world-wide Muslim community, and considers the problems involved in reforming Islamic thought so that it can serve as a more effective basis for unity.

These papers reveal a variety of views regarding the central question raised by the Committee that convened the conference, and those who were invited to discuss them did not agree on an answer. Most of the principal speakers maintained that Islam is actually of quite limited significance in shaping the attitudes and behavior of Muslim states in international relations today, but others differed sharply and few were prepared to dismiss its relevance altogether. It seems clear that a great deal was gained from this confrontation, however. In developing and defending their various positions, the authors have made an important contribution to a better understanding of the complexities involved in defining the contemporary role of Islam and have made it possible for the discussion to continue on a more enlightened basis.

Financial support for this undertaking was provided by the Ford Foundation, and for this we are most thankful. An expression of appreciation is also due to R. Taylor Cole, Provost of Duke University, and to the following members of the Duke University Committee on International Relations for their part in the organization of the conference: David G. Bradley, Joel G. Colton, Robinson O. Everett, John M. Fein, William E. Scott, Patrick R. Vincent, and William P. Yohe (chairman). Neither the Foundation nor the University is responsible, however, for the opinions expressed in this volume. Finally, I wish to acknowledge my indebtedness to my wife; her assistance from beginning to end was invaluable.

Durham, North Carolina J. HARRIS PROCTOR
June, 1964

Contents

ISLAM
and
International
Relations

Religion and Politics in Christianity and Islam

By H. A. R. Gibb

The first question we must ask is whether the subject proposed for this discussion makes sense, and, if so, in what respect? Is there any real (i.e., effective) relation between religion and political action in the modern world?

How are we to define religion in this context? Are we speaking in terms of individual commitment, or of group ideals and aspirations, or of activities, overt or indirect, of organized religious communities and the pressures they exert, or attempt to exert, on political leaders and institutions? Even the skeptic who would deny that religion, as such, has any relation to politics would admit the third, at least, of these alternatives as a real factor. But he might go on, with some show of justice, to ask whether such organized bodies, when they engage in such activities and pressures, are not in fact political bodies, acting for political ends, by no means necessarily identical with the individual religious commitments or the religious ideals and aspirations of their members. He might ask how the spokesmen for Islam reconcile their consciences with the secular implications of nationalist programs, how the actions of organized Zionism can be squared with the insights and teaching of the Hebrew prophets, how, above all, the Christian churches have, in the name of the Prince of Peace, over centuries supported warring nations and factions, and accepted political alliances with Muslims, Hindus, and Shintoists against other Christians.

Whatever apologies may be put forward for these and similar actions, they do nevertheless raise, and raise profoundly, the question whether, when it comes to political action on the grand or international scale, there is any difference at all between the behavior of Muslims, Jews, and Christians, as represented by their organized religious institutions. If then we are going to discover a positive rather than a negative answer to the question, we must shift the focus of discussion to another plane.

To begin with, let us look in brief and general outline at the ideal demands that Christianity and Islam make upon the individual believer, and then at the social institutions by which these demands are supported. Since both religions postulate a personal God, both lay their basic emphasis upon the personal responsibility of the individual to act in accordance with the revealed Will of God, and both prescribe for this purpose a number of ritual duties and a code of moral duty. Performance of ritual duties does not compensate for disregard of the moral obligations, nor does habitual moral behavior compensate for neglect of the ritual duties. The moral duties, at least, are essentially the same in both religions, although the ritual duties are variously structured. In both, the ultimate sanction for right conduct is a Judgment after death, leading either to eternal bliss or eternal damnation.

The major organizational differences between the two religious communities, on the other hand, have developed out of the social and political situations with which they were confronted at the early stages. Christianity arose within a society in which the natural social ties had long since been weakened or had disintegrated, a society in which individuals were related to one another only on a basis of legal principle, which I shall summarily designate as contract. Membership in the church gave to such individuals a new and needed sense of community. Thus the unit of Christian society was the congregation, composed of individuals of diverse occupations and social ranks, subsequently developing into the parish—a territorial segment of town or countryside embracing all its inhabitants under the pastoral care and guidance of an authorized member of the hierarchy. Islam arose within a society of strongly marked and self-conscious kinship groupings, and while it created a supratribal community, its social units continued to be kin-groups. Not only so, but the operation of its moral prescriptions contributed to strengthen their solidarity, and to assimilate other groupings (as in the cities) to kinship groupings.

In both organizations, attitudes toward the political institution were ambivalent, but marked by differences arising out of the differing initial relation of each to the civil power, and consequent internal developments. To attempt to analyze and state conclusions on such a vast topic in a few sentences may be foolhardy, but the risk must be accepted. Briefly, then, the early Christian community, enjoined in principle to be subject to the civil power, found itself in the position of a harried opposition. In order to maintain itself, it needed and created the moral support of a guiding and controlling hierarchy. In the circumstances, as the community expanded in spite of persecutions, the hierarchy was forced to aim at imposing its authority upon the rulers also, and was tempted to use the political power thus acquired for its own ends. For ecclesiastical hierarchy finds it difficult to tolerate a rival; and, while somewhat self-consciously dissociating itself from the civil power, it has time and again sought to use it to root out any "heresy" that challenged its claim to represent the one true Church. Consequently, differences of theological opinion, in producing rival hierarchies, have led to violent conflicts for control of the civil power. The Church of Rome has not to this day repudiated its claim to use the civil power in its support "as of right"; but even minor Protestant conventicles—witness the history of Geneva or of the Bay State—have acted in the same manner when circumstances were in their favor, thereby justifying the skeptic's accusation of their political transformation. Thus Christianity has seldom been free from wars of religion, hot or cold, and the individual Christian has been far less conscious of his fellowship in the Body of Christ with Christians of other denominations than of his membership in a particular communion.

Islam, on the other hand, emerged into the world under a political organization, and its earliest differences of opinion were expressed in the garb of political issues. Its identification with the political leadership was still further emphasized by the accepted obligation to extend the political rule of Islam to the utmost limits and by the actual conflicts that it waged with the outer world. But the sweeping extent of the political victory, extending from Central Asia to Spain, itself raised political problems of the most acute kind: problems of size, of unification, of institutional organisms (administrative and judicial). The early centuries of Islamic history are filled with the conflicts derived from the stresses created by these problems and by the confrontation of diverse social, political, and economic traditions with the now irreversible fact of Islam. In these circumstances, the religious leaders quickly became aware of the dangers implicit in the identification of religion with government; in their need to safeguard the religious values of Islam they were forced therefore to de-emphasize political issues, to loosen their political connections, and, instead of trying to underpin an unattainable and in any case only half-Islamic universal empire, to devote their main efforts to developing a common religious consciousness within a universal Muslim community. The effort to prevent disruption by softening or mediating between political differences was carried over also into doctrinal differences, with the result that, except for isolated instances of religious intransigence, they succeeded in instilling in all Muslims the conviction that they were brethren in one universal community. More strikingly still, although the Christian world constituted the major obstacle to the expansion of Islam, so that its doctrinal rejection of Christianity was confirmed and intensified by an abiding political hostility, the Muslim community, protected from jealousy by its inner conviction of divine election, gave full religious liberty (but not equal citizenship) to Christians and Jews, and never sanctioned pogroms against them on religious grounds.

Along with this, however, the political leaders and some of the religious leaders in Islam were faced with a particular problem by the character of the social groups within the Muslim community. By reason of their natural structure and of the absence of any hierarchical organization, such groups were essentially political, and in considerable measure autonomous within the limits of their respective functions. The problem was to find a principle of sociopolitical integration, and it is in this respect that one of the major differences between the Christian and the Islamic systems becomes manifest.

In the Christian world, the principal factor in this development was the survival of the Roman and Germanic legal institutions alongside, and to a great extent independent of, the ecclesiastical institution. These supplied an organized secular framework for society, based on function and contract, out of which there evolved the modern Western concepts of law and legislative institutions. They also influenced the Christian churches to develop their own systems of ecclesiastical law, with periodical councils, synods, and assemblies. Alongside ecclesiastical discipline, therefore, Western (Christian) man had at his disposal a flexible and pragmatic instrument, which could be and was adapted to changing social situations, but at any given time constituted a normative structure governing his social relations with positive sanctions.

In contrast to this, Islam arose in a society whose only notion of law was established custom and tradition, sanctioned by public opinion. To this, Islam added the concept of positive law as divine ordinance through revelation and, with the substitution of Prophetic for tribal custom and tradition, combined all three in elaborating its Sacred Law, the *Sharī'ah.* Its basis in revelation gave it the character of an absolute and theoretically immutable system, except where the Law itself allowed for minor variations in practice. It was also theoretically all-inclusive, leaving no room for any other structure of law or legislation. Owing to the persistence of this theoretical structure, Islam gives the appearance of a monolithic and static structure, and is often presented as such. But in reality, even in the field of doctrine and ethics, it has never remained immobile, but has evolved through the centuries. Even more inevitable, therefore, was the evolution of its legal and social institutions, although without breaching the overarching unity. Because the Law became the central unifying institution in Islam, it acquired a quasi-political character, and religious practice and morality received a legalistic stamp. This was deplored in deeply religious circles, but it had extremely important consequences. While on the one hand, the Law in the abstract continued to be elaborated in an ideal direction, without regard to historical or other circumstances, its theoretical uniformity concealed, on the other hand, a fair degree of elasticity in practice through the application of juristic casuistry to a variety of situations in different regions, even to the extent of ignoring or voiding some of its provisions in the daily affairs and legal practice of a far from ideal community (a development to which specialists in Islamic Law have as yet given regrettably little attention).

We are here concerned more particularly with the results of this activity in the area of political institutions. Since the Law was all-inclusive, it should in principle have defined also the modalities of Islamic government and the mutual relations and responsibilities of governors and governed. In fact, however, it went no further than to define in broad general terms the particular responsibilities and moral duties attaching to the *function* of the governors. Otherwise, the Law assumed their relations with the governed to be subsumed under the general categories of Muslim social conduct, in much the same way as the basic fiscal obligations of the Muslim were assumed to be confined to his payment of alms-tax. Apart from this broad formal definition, there is no "political theory" in Islam—that is to say, no discussion of the means by which these ideal ends were to be safeguarded, even when the processes of history, into which we need not enter, soon proved both of these assumptions to be inadequate. The gap was filled among the Sunnīs by conditional condonation of the historical process, and among the Shīʿah by a resigned acceptance of usurping governments pending the appearance of the divinely guided Mahdī. Both amounted to much the same thing in practice. The essential duties of the governor were clear: to protect the territories and religious institutions of the community and to respect the general principles of Muslim conduct, not imposing penal or other sanctions beyond those required for the performance of his political functions. But although some modern Muslim theorists have argued that Islamic principles demand something like a modern democratic structure of government, the plain fact is that neither prescription nor history called for effective participation by individual members or organized groups of the community in the political responsibilities of the rulers; even the religious leaders, as we have seen, were hesitant or unwilling to become involved in the practical affairs of government. Therefore, both in theory and in practice, all civil and judicial authority was derived by delegation from the ruler, and was revocable by him at will. The civil duty of the subject was obedience, his religious duty to use his influence for good within his sphere of action; only when the Faith itself was in danger had he the right, under proper leadership, to resort to force.

Let me re-emphasize the point. The religious leaders of Islam had quickly been forced to learn the lesson that political issues must always divide men from one another—unless indeed the government should be of such transcendent virtue as to satisfy all the diverse interpretations of the ideal. Since governments in practice fall far short of perfect virtue, and their policies are clouded by worldly interests and ambitions, the spiritual health of the community could be safeguarded only by avoiding all personal commitment to and contamination by the agencies and the hirelings of political power. Was this, then, "moral irresponsibility"? Surely not. These leaders saw their field of responsible action in the integration of all the diverse social and racial groups in the Islamic world into a community of common faith; and to achieve this unity the religious and social life of the community had to be protected from the dangers of involvement in political issues.

The counterpart of this, on the other hand, was that political life was set free to follow its own rhythms and necessities, and these in turn were inevitably determined by the incidence of power. The evolution by which Islamic government became completely identified with military power did not, however, in spite of encroachments in economic life and occasional local tyrannies, change the basic relations and division of functions between the political and the religious institutions. What resulted from this situation was a series of mutual compromises. No established government in Islam, however autocratic, failed to respect the religious ordinances and personal law of Islam, or to preserve a connecting link with the religious institution by appointing official judges (*qādīs*) to the Muslim courts and associating a body of religious leaders with its administration. In return for this, these religious leaders were charged with the task of so mediating between the ideal demands of the Law and the actual policies and exigencies of the governors as to preserve the unity and religious heritage of the community.

And yet, in our history books, Muslim governments often present the appearance of models of arbitrary and unrestrained autocracy. We are apt to forget, however, the prevalent and increasing violence within large sectors of Islamic society due to the expansion of nomadism in Western Asia and North Africa, especially from the tenth century onward —a trend that infected agricultural and urban life as well, and was reversed only in the nineteenth century. In face of this, even the most orthodox jurists (an ibn-Taimīyah, for example) were forced to admit the inadequacy of ordinary religious jurisdictions and to recognize the right, even the duty, of the ruler and his agents to exercise summary justice. The extravagant lengths to which this was sometimes carried went, no doubt, far beyond the intentions and the approval of the jurists, but in this, as in so many other cases, they were compelled, little by little, to admit, or to condone, derogations from the letter of the Law in the interests of administrative practice and political stability.

is function of the official *'ulamā'*, however, even if it enabled the community and its religious organisms to adapt themselves to (or at least to coexist with) successive political and administrative developments, was recognized for what it was, and did not affect the ambivalence of public attitudes to the political institution. On the one hand, despite all the imperfections of the governors, government as such retained something of a moral aura as the defender of the interests and religious values of the community–usually personified in the ruler himself; on the other hand, its administrative regulations and exactions on land, industry, and persons, and the processes resorted to by its officers were regarded as arbitrary and without authority in themselves, and directed only to the furthering of their private interests. In the eyes of the governed, official "justice" was no justice. The only authoritative Law is that of Islam; everything else is merely temporary (and more or less forced) accommodation to the whims of a changing constellation of political overlords. This distinction between authority and power is fundamental for an understanding of the Muslim attitude toward government. The contrast between these conceptions and the medieval European theory of the Two Swords needs no elaboration. Since government based on military power has no stability or authority in itself, anything more than a *de facto* recognition would be a derogation from the absolute rights of the Law, and any attempt to introduce constitutional reforms would be ineffective.

To conclude this argument: In any historic community, its political institution, however constituted, and whether its constitution be written or unwritten, will in the long run be so structured as to protect and subserve its central values. The Muslim community was no exception. Its central concern was not the structure of government, but the preservation of the system of religious and moral duties elaborated in the Law, and the "rights" of the individual "to life, liberty and the pursuit of happiness" were conditional upon his performance of these duties.

But what reason is there to believe that the actual forms and institutions of government in Christian and Islamic history are anything more than tangentially related to the explicit doctrines of their respective religions? One might almost say, indeed, that in the development of their political and religious institutions Islam and Christianity display a curious cross-division. The moral responsibility of the individual is as strongly emphasized in Islam as in Christianity. If his political responsibility has somehow or other a significantly Christian value, is it not strange that it took the Christian world 1,700 years to discover it, and that 200 years later it is still so precarious in many Christian countries? Surely the most that can be said is that certain Christian virtues have found an explicit focus of expression in adopting certain ideas which—like law—entered into the Christian world from other sources, and that having adopted these ideas the Christian world has raised them to a higher moral potential (not always, unhappily, realized in practice).

The spotlight of comparison between the two communities in the field of government would therefore focus on the secular elements present in them respectively, and the social mechanics by which these elements can be developed and related to the religious structure. In order to "explain" their contrasts, we should be compelled to penetrate, not only below the dogmatic to the sociolegal level, but even below these norms to more profound depths. Such an attempt is all the more obligatory because the religious structures themselves reveal a diversity of underlying psychological attitudes, and because in any consideration of their consequences for political action, the decisive factor is more likely to be the psychological attitudes related to and expressed in their religious organizations than the doctrinal positions and institutional actions of the organizations themselves. Necessary as this investigation is, however, it is not within my competence to undertake it; and rather than indulge in what would be pure guesswork I shall continue the argument on the evidence of the more easily observable indices.

Granted that the revival of Roman civil law in Western Europe supplied a body of ideas and a more flexible instrument than theocratic or revealed law, we still have to ask the question *why* it was revived in Europe. Surely not as a mere scholastic pastime; but because it met some need that was beginning to be felt in social life and organization, largely (though not wholly) arising out of the developing economic organisms. Yet fairly similar economic groups existed also in the Muslim world at that time, and they felt no such need. It can only be suggested that the European groups possessed no natural force of cohesion, and therefore sought to supply it by a system of contractual relations both between themselves and with the political and ecclesiastical authorities. In the Muslim world, on the other hand, the challenge presented by autocracy produced its own appropriate response. This was developed out of older roots in the social economy of the Arab and Middle Eastern populations. Just as the Arab tribes and clans retained their social solidarity, so new institutions of social solidarity grew up in the cities among the artisans, the tradesmen, and ultimately among all the professional classes. The strength of the kin-groups among the tribesmen and of craft and professional guilds (themselves often reinforced by kinship ties) among the townsmen gave an inner resilience to the society, and even a certain measure of protection to their members, while remaining resistant to any legal subjection to an external authority. Thanks to the centuries-old efforts of the religious leaders, these small closed groups, jealous of one another and of their internal autonomy, had already been brought to recognize a common divine Law. Some of the credit for this, no doubt, may be due to the long tradition of divinely enacted law in the Near East, and it must be recalled that they often found ways and means of adapting the jurists' constructions of the Law to their own interests and requirements—for example, in banking and capital transactions. It was the great merit of the Sūfi (or mystical) fraternities that they strengthened the vigor of the guilds by their linking up of the guilds with the religious institution and thus interlocking the guilds to a certain extent with one another. But the jealous watch maintained by the governors upon any organizations that might challenge their autocratic powers prevented the guilds from developing (as they developed in Western Europe) as potential political forces, or at least as checks upon the unlimited caprice of local potentates.

Indeed, the Sūfi movements, in their all-embracing expansion in the later centuries, themselves reinforced the separation of the political institutions and the socioreligious organization of the Muslim community. For the negative side of Sūfism, in its disregard for merely material objects and concerns, had the effect of pushing certain tendencies within the Islamic community to their extremes, with the natural consequence of a certain loss of inner balance. Among these tendencies was the refusal of involvement in political activities, and I should go so far as to say that this extreme political apathy inculcated by Sūfism furnished one of the conditions for the modern political revolution in the Muslim world.

The other condition was furnished by the inefficiency of the actual governments, *in Islamic terms.* As already pointed out, the function of Islamic government was to protect the Muslim community and its institutions from external and internal aggression. Note that these were the *minimum* functions that entitled it to claim the obedience of its subjects. Its major function had been to serve as the dynamic spearhead of the Muslim community, to maintain it in continuous forward movement; only so did it deserve, and gain, the complete loyalty of its Muslim population. As it ceased to advance and became politically inert, inner cohesion weakened. In earlier centuries, the normal reaction to this was its replacement by a more vigorous military regime. By the nineteenth century, however, not only was this no longer possible, in face of European restraint, but, more serious, every Muslim government had shown itself incapable of protecting its territories from external aggression and had lost its moral basis.

The outcome of this situation is well known. On the one hand, the governing groups, in their search for means to overcome the disparity of power between Europe and the Islamic world, not only reorganized their military forces on the European model, but also aimed to strengthen themselves internally by introducing Western administrative institutions and systems of law. Because of the general political apathy they were able to do this with little opposition. Some of the reforms, indeed, met with general approval, notably the putting of an end to the arbitrary powers of life and death exercised by subordinate officers, and the establishment of regular criminal courts, applying a definite criminal code. On the other hand, those religious leaders who, a little later, became aware of the disruptive possibilities of some of the political and legal innovations to the ideal of the Muslim community could in the political field do little more than fight a rearguard action in defense of the traditional Islamic institutions. For, in face of the threat or actuality of Western domination, intramural disputes necessarily took second place, lest they weaken the common cause of Muslim resistance and self-determination. Consequently, even when aware of the blatant exploitation of Islam for political purposes, the religious leaders have been willy-nilly involved in an alliance with their local political movements and governments, whether absolutist, constitutional, nationalist, or, as in Egypt today, "Arab socialist." Yet, in one respect at least, they have been mending their fences, since, having rightly recognized a major source of the weak resistance of the Muslim community in the Sūfi attitude, they set themselves to uproot the influence of the Sūfi organizations—a step which incidentally completed the disruption of the craft corporations, although it is more difficult to determine what effect this had temporarily on the spiritual life of the community.

With the wildfire spread of the new legal and administrative institutions, however, culminating in the introduction of constitutional governments, the Muslim countries had, to all appearances at least, caught up with the West in their political institutions. In view of what has been said, it seems clear that this achievement had been bought at a price. That price was the weakening of the old forces of cohesion, in some cases to the point of extinction. The new legal institutions found their main support in the new commercial and professional classes, for whom they met the same need as for their predecessors in Western Europe. For the older sections of Muslim society, they meant little more than a new set of arbitrary regulations propounded by a new governing class, and were as devoid of authority as those of earlier governments. At a deeper level, much the same may be said of the new doctrines of nationalism. In seeking to create a new binding force between the multiple groups within each state, they seem to threaten the deep sense of unity within the Muslim community, and to implicate it in the rivalries and ambitions of secular political forces.

Such rivalries are, of course, no novelty in Islamic history. In the early centuries, revolts and civil wars were conducted under the banner of rival sectarian interpretations of Islam. But as the sense of religious community became more deeply rooted, their political aspect predominated, to the point that they became mere dynastic conflicts, irrelevant to the community as a whole. Even in the long struggle between the Ottoman and Persian empires, it is doubtful how far Sunnī and Shī'ī antagonism was engaged, except in the disputed province of Iraq. As between Sunnīs themselves, there are two features of the last two centuries that seem particularly significant. Firstly, the two successful native revolts against the Ottoman Empire were conducted under the banner of Islamic order—those of the Wahhabīs and the Sanūsīs. Of the other two revolts, Muḥammad 'Alī's war with the Ottomans was a dynastic conflict; the Arab Revolt of 1916 would probably never have got off the ground without Turkey's involvement in the European War and British encouragement and support, and was at the time seen far more as a bid for power by the sharīfs than as a national rising—hence its sequel, a third successful religious war in Arabia.

Secondly, since the establishment of the national states in the Near East, while there have been revolutions or revolts in almost every one of them, and while verbal warfare and subversion have been violent at times, no actual fighting has taken place between them (except briefly between Saudi Arabia and Yemen). No doubt, if war were to break out, the national armies would obey the orders of their leaders. But those leaders are well aware that it would be regarded by the mass of their peoples as a fratricidal conflict, however it might be camouflaged by political (or even religious) slogans at the moment. That no government can with impunity disregard the strength of popular feeling on this point is shown by the degree to which all of them are committed to the principle of Arab unity as an article of national faith.

This drive for Arab unity may be explained, and with justice, as an expression of Arab nationalism. But it would be a serious error to identify the character and roots of Arab nationalism with those of Western nationalism. There can be no doubt of the influence of Western doctrines upon the intelligentsia, more especially, I suggest, in generating and sustaining concepts of regional nationalism; but even so, the Western ideas were and remain superimposed upon a foundation of old-established attitudes. How deeply the secular roots of nationalism have penetrated into the general Arab mind cannot be exactly established; but whatever their depth, they coexist and interact with the whole body of inherited forms of thought, and its intellectual content is necessarily influenced by this fact. All competent observers are agreed that among the components of Arab nationalism, one of the strongest and most pervasive is Islam. The Arabs cannot be deprived of their history or of the emotional forces bound up with it.

I am not going to argue here the relative weight of secular and religious elements in Arab nationalism—a question the answer to which differs in any case with different groups. It is significant, however, that in spite of the unfriendly attitudes of Turkish and Iranian nationalists toward the Arabs, the idea of war with Turkey or Iran is as "unthinkable" to Arab nationalists as an inter-Arab war. The point I wish to stress is that even within Arab nationalism, in the broad sense—and notwithstanding the programs of particular parties—there is ample evidence that the traditional Muslim attitude toward government still exerts a powerful influence. This is one of the factors that underlies the success of President Jamāl 'Abd al-Nāṣir, and that I suspect he fully realizes and turns to account. To see in him only the military "strong man" idolized by the mob is to see the external appearance without the inner force. In his recent pronouncements on "Arab socialism" he is not only building, however tentatively and pragmatically, on a general foundation of "welfare-state philosophy" derived from the West, but is also relating this to Islamic ideas of egalitarianism and social responsibility, seeing rightly that by giving his program an Islamic significance, this provides an acceptable ground for a more explicit socialist policy. And in so reformulating these ideas in a new sense and a new context, in restating the meaning of history for his people, he at the same time wipes the slate clean of the nagging memory of past Islamic compromises.

Above all, however, he is re-establishing the function of the

Muslim government as a moral enterprise, and the position of the Muslim ruler as the person who is charged with protecting and furthering the welfare of his subjects. Of course, this is expressed not in the traditional terms, but in the contemporary idiom; what underlies it is a conception (I quote from a recent article by Malcolm Kerr)

> characterized by a moral preference—not just a tactical preference—for maintaining the maximum degree of unity of purpose and action at all political and social levels; by an emphasis upon the virtues of group solidarity and the evils of individual self-absorption and self-seeking; by a mistrust of competition, bargaining, and the promotion of special interests; and by a vision of strong government as a liberator rather than a danger to liberty. The free individual is not primarily a man who is left alone to do as he sees fit, but one whose usefulness and security in society are assured.[1]

The liberal ideas derived from nineteenth-century Europe are openly discarded, not only as irrelevant to present needs, but as leading to "social, economic, and political exploitation" in the interests of selfish minorities, and to discord and class conflict. The persistent Islamic ideal of social unity, with its emphasis on the evils of division, swings easily into line against the institutionalization of dissension and conflict represented by Western democracy. Its traditional linking of rights with duties militates against the abuse of wealth in virtue of supposed "natural" or legal rights. The new doctrine gives shape and content to the profound conviction (which haunted even the "liberal" thinkers) that the West, for all its discoveries and material progress, does not possess the secret of the good life. Thus the intelligentsia who patronized the experiment of constitutional government are ruthlessly swept aside, except insofar as they are willing to serve the new objectives of the socialist state.

Although this development has been most forcibly demonstrated by the revolutionary government in Egypt, the tendencies that it illustrates are too clearly present in other Muslim countries from West Africa to Indonesia to be regarded as singular. The question that it raises is whether or how far this new kind of authoritarian government will preserve or interpret the essential Muslim principles and values. Up to the present, it seems in its overt legislation and activities to be pulling down the traditional Muslim institutions; but although the overt facts are not in dispute, it is much less certain that they express the inner reality. It is true that the ancient and deep-rooted distrust continues among the masses of the governed; everything that is touched by the finger of government is suspect. The more al-Azhar is exploited as a trump card for Islamic propaganda, the more vulnerable it becomes in Muslim public opinion and the less useful, therefore, for all of its purposes, good or bad. Yet, in the search, conscious or unconscious, for giving some deeper justification and emotional drive to "Arab socialism," the political leaders have to link their policies with the only system of universal ideas congenial to the minds of their people, i.e., Islam. But they are no longer tied to the medieval institutions and interpretations; in their new legislation they are beneficiaries of the programs of Islamic reform propagated by earlier "liberals" and Muslim revivalists, who attacked the stagnant traditionalism and obscurantism of the past and prepared the way for the changes they are introducing. It can be said that they are gambling with the future, in the expectation or hope that out of the confrontation with the modern world and a reconstructed social order there will emerge a new and acceptable interpretation of Islam, patterned on the lines of their experiment and furnishing emotional support for it.

It is, no doubt, scarcely conceivable that the existing religious communities and institutions will emerge from the tremendous crises of mankind, proceeding and still to come, without substantial change—but equally inconceivable that in the next century or two either Christianity or Islam will be superseded. Of course, one cannot foresee in what directions religious thought will move in the future, or what the relations of the institutional religions will be with the political regimes. But so far as Islam is concerned, the observer cannot but be impressed by the revision and rethinking (which are not the same thing, however) of the traditional Islamic positions which are in process in most of the Muslim countries. Such legal reforms as the new laws applying to marriage, divorce, inheritance, are bound to leave a permanent mark on Islamic society. So also the formal pronouncements of Muslim religious leaders (of the kind cited by Professor Vatikiotis) on the adaptation of Qur'ānic principles to a reconstructed social order are laying new foundations in a practical sense—even granting that they are to be regarded on much the same footing as the official pronouncements of earlier generations of Muslim *'ulamā'* to mediate between *Sharī'ah* principles and political innovations.

What is disturbing in the present situation in Egypt, however, as well as under other authoritarian regimes, is the inert condition of religious thought (at least in public expression) and the passivity with which the religious leaders no longer lead, but consent to play the subordinate (and sometimes humiliating) role of "ad-men" for their governments. Where "Arab socialism" has broken with the thought of both religious revivalism and liberalism is in repressing or bypassing their common doctrine of *personal* activism and dynamic purpose and creativity. The contrast between this situation and the vigorous and creative thought devoted by Muslim scholars in India and Pakistan to the more fundamental religious problems involved in a revision of *Sharī'ah* rules is both striking and depressing. But the future of Islam does not depend upon current developments in Egypt, perhaps fortunately. While both of these developments, that illustrated by Egypt and that in India and Pakistan, have a certain community of aim in removing the dead hand of medievalism, the next stage of Islamic history may well be focused upon the conflict or convergence between the two forces making for reconstruction: those of personal religious endeavor, striving to rebuild a dynamic Islamic community, and those of governmental regulation, seeking to restrict its role to that of an auxiliary motor.

So far as the external relations of Islam are concerned, it would seem, as of now, that the violent conflicts of the past between Islam and Christianity have been replaced by a stage, if not of mutual recognition, at least of mutual acquiescence in the abandonment of force. But the rivalry continues, most actively in Africa, and there are ample indications that, whatever the outcome of the confrontation of internal forces that I have just analyzed, the traditional linking of Islam to social and political activity persists, and will continue. I am not prophesying the revival of an overtly militant Islam, but among the unknown range of possibilities now being produced by contemporary stresses in every continent, one that the West would be wise not to discount is the re-emergence of a revived and reconstructed Islam as a world factor.

NOTE

1. "Arab Radical Notions of Democracy," *St. Antony's Papers, No. 16: Middle Eastern Affairs, Number Three,* ed. Albert Hourani (London, 1963), pp. 10–11.

The Islamic Theory of International Relations and Its Contemporary Relevance

By Majid Khadduri

In order to reconstruct the Islamic theory of international relations, we should recall that Islam is not merely a set of religious ideas and practices, but also a political community endowed with a system of law designed to protect the collective interests of believers as well as to regulate their relations with the outside world. The basic assumption underlying Islam's external relations with other nations is the principle that only the community of believers is the subject of the Islamic legal and ethical system, while all other communities are the object of that system, although the latter communities are by no means denied certain advantages of the Islamic system. The ultimate objective of Islam was to establish peace within the territory brought under the pale of its public order and to expand the area of the validity of that order to include the entire world.

Before Islam could achieve that ultimate objective, it had to enter into relations with communities that had not yet submitted to its control in accordance with a set of rules and practices. Conformity to Islamic legal and ethical standards was required not only of the believers who had come under Islamic sovereignty, but also of believers whose territory had not yet been brought under Islamic rule. For Islam as a religion expanded beyond the frontiers of the state and the believers owed their legal—though not necessarily their political—allegiance to Islam. However, the non-Muslims who resided within the Islamic community, although they were regarded as the subjects of the state (though not members of the religious community), were not bound by all the Islamic ethical and legal rules. Islamic authority, however, had to deal with the problems arising from their interrelationships with Muslims.

In Islamic legal theory, the world was therefore divided into two divisions: *dār al-Islām* (*Pax Islamica*), comprising Islamic and non-Islamic territories held under Islamic sovereignty, and the rest of the world, called *dār al-ḥarb*, or the "territory of war." The first included the community of believers as well as those who entered into an alliance with Islam. The inhabitants of those territories were either Muslims, who formed the community of believers, and non-Muslims of the tolerated religions (Christians, Jews, and others known to have possessed Scriptures), who preferred to hold fast to their own law and religion at the price of paying a poll tax (*jizyah*) to Muslim authority. The Muslims enjoyed full rights of citizenship, while the followers of the tolerated religions enjoyed only partial civil rights; but all enjoyed full status as subjects of the caliph, the head of state, in their claim both to internal security and protection from foreign attack. The caliph, in the discharge of his responsibilities in foreign relations, spoke in the name of all subjects. The relations between the Islamic and non-Islamic communities within the Islamic legal superstructure were regulated in accordance with special charters, originally issued by the caliphs, recognizing the canon law of each tolerated community bearing on matters of personal status. The world surrounding the Islamic political community was known as the *dār al-ḥarb,* because it remained beyond the pale of *Pax Islamica.* It lacked the legal competence to enter into intercourse with Islam on the basis of equality and reciprocity. Such territory may therefore be regarded as in a "state of nature," because it failed to conform to Islam's ethical and legal standards. Some Muslim publicists, especially Shāfi'ī jurists, devised a third temporary division of the world, called *dār al-ṣulḥ* (territory of peaceful arrangement) or *dār al-'ahd* (territory of covenant), giving qualified recognition to non-Islamic communities if they entered into treaty relations with Islam, on conditions agreed upon between the two parties (provided Islam was paid an annual tribute). The Ḥanafī jurists, however, never recognized the existence of a third division of the world, arguing that if the inhabitants of a territory concluded a peace treaty and paid a tribute, it became part of the *Pax Islamica* and its people were entitled to the protection of Islam, because otherwise it would be part of the *dār al-ḥarb* and an object of Islam.

The *dār al-Islām* was in theory in a state of war with the *dār al-ḥarb* because the ultimate objective of Islam was the world. If *dār al-ḥarb* were reduced by Islam, Islamic public order would supersede other orders, and non-Muslim communities either accept Islam or submit to Islamic sovereignty in accordance with certain provisions agreed upon in a constitutional charter or in a treaty which by no means would be regarded as between two equal parties. The *dār al-ḥarb,* however, was not regarded as a no man's land, even though it remained outside the pale of Islamic public order. It was entitled to conduct its hostile relations with Islam in accordance with the rules set forth in Islamic law governing the state of war between Muslim and non-Muslim communities. Thus the Muslim was under obligation to respect the rights of non-Muslims, both combatants and civilians, while fighting was in progress. Moreover, during the short intervals of peace, when hostilities were in suspense either by a truce or peace treaty the duration of which could not in theory exceed ten years, Islam took cognizance of the authority or authorities that existed in countries that had not yet been brought under Islamic sovereignty. But this cognizance of the need of authority in the *dār al-ḥarb* did not constitute *recognition,* in the modern sense of the term, because recognition would have implied Islam's acceptance of non-Islamic sovereignties as equal entities under the Islamic system. Islam's cognizance of non-Islamic sovereignties merely meant that authority was, by nature, necessary for the survival of political communities, even when they existed in the state of nature. It follows that if a Muslim were traveling or domiciled in the *dār al-ḥarb,* he should not oppose the authority of that territory, unless charged with the duty of so doing by a specific order from Islamic authority. If the Muslim entered the *dār al-ḥarb* by a pledge of security (*amān*) he was under obligation to respect the law and authority of that territory and abstain from committing an offense or injury to non-Muslims, so long as he enjoyed the benefits of the pledge of security. He was also under obligation to conform to his own law, but if there were conflicts between his own law and the law of that territory, there was no doubt as to what his choice must be.

However, the state of war between the two territories should not always take the form of actual hostilities; for, if fighting came to an end, the state of war would be reduced to what we call in modern international practice a state of nonrecognition, that is, the incompetence of the *dār al-ḥarb* to possess a legal status under Islamic law so long as it failed to conform to Islam's legal and ethical standards or attain the status of the tolerated religious communities. But, this state of nonrecognition did not imply, as in the modern sense of the term, the impossibility of conducting direct negotiation or concluding treaties. Such actions were considered neither to imply equality between the two parties nor necessarily to possess a permanent character. Probably the nearest equivalent to this situation in international practice is the recognition of insurgency which does not preclude later *de facto* or *de jure* recognition or approval of the regime's conduct under insurgency. It merely means that an authority to enforce law and order in a certain territory during a rebellion or civil war was necessary in these circumstances. Thus the Islamic state, in entering into diplomatic negotiation with a non-Islamic state, did not intend to recognize it—that is, to extend the advantages of Islamic law to non-Islamic areas—but rather to admit tacitly that a certain authority or authorities were necessary in the countries of the *dār al-ḥarb,* so long as they remained outside the pale of Islamic sovereignty.

The instrument through which the *dār al-ḥarb* would be transformed into the *Pax Islamica* was the *jihād.* But *jihād,* in the broad sense of the term, did not necessarily mean war or fighting, even though a state of war theoretically existed between Islamic and non-Islamic countries, since the expansion of the *Pax Islamica* might be achieved by peaceful as well as by violent means. The *jihād* was equivalent to the Christian concept of the crusade—a war of words as well as of the sword. To Muslim publicists it was an "exertion" of one's own power to make the word of Allah supreme over the world, and the individual's recompense would be the achievement of salvation, because participation in the *jihād,* especially by martyrdom, was Allah's direct way to paradise.[1] This participation might be fulfilled by the heart, by the tongue, by the hands, and by the sword. The *jihād* was accordingly a form of religious propaganda carried out by spiritual as well as by material means.[2] No other form of war was permitted, since Islam prohibited all kinds of war save that in the fulfillment of Islam's ultimate purpose. The *jihād* in Islam, as the crusade in Western Christendom, was the *bellum justum.*[3] In Islam, however, the *jihād* was closely associated with authority, to be employed for *raisons d'état.* For inherent in the state's action in waging a *jihād* was the establishment of Islamic sovereignty, and the expansion of the area of the validity of Allah's words implied necessarily the establishment of his political authority. As *bellum justum* the *jihād* was a permanent obligation upon Muslims collectively, until the *dār al-ḥarb* would be reduced to nonexistence. The ultimate establishment of *Pax Islamica,* with its all-embracing public order, was a duty imposed on the believers to be carried out by a continuous process of warfare, psychological and political if not strictly military.

II

The Islamic theory of international relations is to be found neither in the Qur'ān nor in the Prophet Muḥammad's utterances, although its basic assumptions were derived from these authoritative sources. It was rather the product of Muslim speculation at a time when the Islamic Empire had reached its full development. Having incorporated a complex of ethnic and cultural groups, Muslim thinkers conceived of Islam as an ecumenical society and formulated a theory of state rationalizing existing conditions and aspirations. Since Islam was still on the move and Muslims possessed vigor and vitality, the state, as the instrument of a universal religion, was considered capable of expanding *ad infinitum*.

But in its early development the state was not universal in character—although religion was conceived of as ecumenical—nor did the state preserve the structure of a universal state in later centuries. From its beginning, the state passed through various stages of evolution, culminating in a golden age of ascendancy often referred to as the Islamic classical period (during which the Islamic theory of external relations was formulated), and then began to accommodate itself to conditions surrounding it until it was finally incorporated in the modern community of nations. The stages through which the Islamic state evolved may be stated as follows:

1. City-state stage	A.D. 622–32
2. The imperial stage	632–750
3. The universal stage	750–*c.*900
4. The "decentralization" stage	*c.*900–*c.*1500
5. The "fragmentation" stage	*c.*1500–1918
6. National stage	1918–

In the middle of the eighth century of the Christian era the Islamic state, having undergone a revolution that changed its internal structure, began to take the shape of a universal state. Previously it had quickly been transformed from an aggregate of city-states grouped together by the Prophet Muḥammad, to an empire made up of Arabs and non-Arab subjects, ruled by the Prophet's early successors and held by Arab legions.[4] From the middle of the eighth to the tenth centuries, the Islamic state became to all intents and purposes truly universal in character. If the Islamic state, during the Golden Age, had resisted the forces working for its transformation into a universal state and failed to conform to the ecumenical character of religion, it would probably have been broken into two or more political entities. Its transformation from an imperial to a universal structure preserved the outward unity of Islam.

However, though the Islamic state recognized in theory no state other than itself, it had to accept certain limitations and accommodate itself to the realities of surrounding conditions. Unable to incorporate the whole of mankind, the state tacitly accepted the principle of coexistence with other states and conducted its external relations in accordance with principles derived not only from Islamic doctrine, but also from its long experiences with other states. The acceptance of the principle of coexistence compelled Islam to accept territorial limitations. Consequently the law was bound to become territorial as well as personal.

Moreover, the Islamic state had undergone changes in its internal structure resulting partly from territorial segregation but mainly from a long conflict between centrifugal and centripetal forces. For a long time there was a controversy as to the nature of authority between two schools of thought, one advocating a monistic theory of authority and another a pluralistic theory. The advocates of the one central authority, represented by leading orthodox writers, argued that since there was one God, the source of all power, and one law (the *Sharī'ah*), there must be one caliph and one authority. The pluralistic school, or the advocates of the division of Islam into two (or more) political entities, argued that whenever Islamic territory is divided by the sea (which may be reformulated as natural barriers), it should split into two (or more) political entities, each headed by a separate caliph and each to enforce the sacred law in his own realm. The latter school of thought was rejected by leading writers, but the former was modified to permit the rise of subentities, governed by heads who were to acknowledge the overlordship of the central caliphate. This compromise, advocated by writers in favor of the decentralization of authority, was first represented by the jurist al-Māwardī (974–1058) who, although in theory emphasizing the ultimate authority of the caliph, tried to adjust the monistic theory of the caliphate to the realities of the political conditions of his time.

After a long period of decentralization, the empire became internally divided into several political entities. Such division kept recurring, but the most lasting one was that which took place at the opening of the sixteenth century when two powerful dynasties—the Ottoman and Ṣafawī—after a long period of conflict relegated their doctrinal differences to the domestic level and recognized the sovereign attributes of one another. This situation became possible after the extinction of the 'Abbāsid dynasty (1258), which represented the ecumenical character of Islamic polity. Its collapse, resulting in the disappearance of the ultimate caliphal authority which it had symbolized, created a vacuum in the Islamic world. For a long while, from the thirteenth to the sixteenth centuries, the Islamic world abounded in political entities, small and great; but the outcome of this anarchy, in which many a state fought battles of life and death, was the emergence of two principal Islamic states—the Ottoman and Persian—each rationalizing its existence by advocating one of the two principal Islamic creeds, the Sunnī and Shī'ī. This was the first lasting territorial division, coinciding with the absorption of the peripheries of Islam by neighboring powers.[5] The fragmentation of Islam, whether regretted as the breakdown of a great ecumenical society or hailed as the progressive evolution of a public order in quest of adapting itself to the ever-changing conditions of life, was necessary if the state were to survive in this world.

III

The incorporation of Islam by the expanding community of nations took place during the nineteenth century, although diplomatic intercourse between Muslim and Christian states had been maintained for a very long time before that century. Christendom and Islam, after a long period of competition and warfare by virtue of which each came to the inevitable conclusion that its legal and political systems could not be imposed on the other, began to adapt themselves to conditions and surroundings permitting the coexistence of more than one potential world order. The implicit acceptance of compromises and toleration made possible the development of rules and principles derived not from religious doctrine but from common interests. Islamic and Christian states passed through a long transitional period of coexistence, which the Spanish Don Manuel in the thirteenth century characterized as *guerra fria* (cold war), until they agreed to conduct their relations on the basis of equality and mutual interests. Islam learned from experience that its conduct of external relations could not be governed for a very long time on the basis of religious doctrine. Its theory of international relations was by necessity subjected to a thorough re-examination on the basis of historical experiences. New principles modifying the Islamic classical doctrines of external relations were bound to develop. It was owing to these modifications that the Islamic states were able to become members of the family of nations and participate in international councils.

The first and the most revolutionary change was the adoption of the principle of peaceful relationship among nations of different religions, replacing the classical principle of the *jihād,* or the permanent state of war between Islamic and non-Islamic lands. The *jihād,* which had entered in practice into a period of suspension, became no longer adequate as the basis of Islam's relationship with other nations. Muslim rulers, especially during the period of fragmentation, made treaties establishing peace with non-Muslim states extending beyond the ten-year period provided under the sacred law.

The most notable instrument that formalized the peaceful relationship between Islam and non-Muslim states was the treaty of 1535. It not only laid down the principle of peace and mutual respect between Sultan Sulaymān the Magnificent and the King of France but also offered it to other Christian princes who were willing to adhere to the treaty (articles 1 and 15). This treaty may be regarded as a point of departure that contributed not only to the recognition of nations of different faiths by Islam, but also to the final incorporation of Muslim and Christian states by the community of nations.

The second fundamental change was the acceptance of the principle of the separation of religious doctrine from the conduct of external relations. This principle, relegating religion to the domestic level, was the product of schism in the creed of Islam. Doctrinal schism was not a new phenomenon in the history of Islam; it was, indeed, recurrent and had resulted in the rise of rival religious-political parties. But no permanent territorial division had resulted from doctrinal schism. At the opening of the sixteenth century, however, a permanent split took place which divided Islam into three zones. The rise of two rival dynasties—the Ottoman and Persian—each advocating a different creed, compelled them after a long period of conflict to separate their doctrinal differences from the conduct of external relations and to regulate their relations on a nonsectarian (i.e., secular) basis. The separation between religious doctrine and the conduct of external relations within Islam was not unlike the split of Christianity into two sects—Catholic and Protestant—resulting from religious warfare, and the agreement among Christian princes to relegate religious doctrine to the domestic level and to conduct their external relations on a secular basis. The principle *cuius regio, eius religio,* first adopted at the Peace of Augsburg in 1555, became the basis of the Peace of Westphalia (1648) and an accepted principle governing first the relationship among the Christian states of Europe and later among states of different faiths throughout the world.

The third important change was the adoption by Islam of the principles of territorial sovereignty and territorial law necessitated by territorial segregation. Like the medieval Christian concepts of state and law, the classical Islamic state was universal and its law personal, not territorial. For in a state which is potentially capable of embracing the world and has its law laid down by a Supreme Legislator, territorial limitations are irrelevant. The allegiance of men would be to symbols of unity, not to territorial divisions. However, when a universal state suffered a split in its body politic under the changing conditions of modern life, the constituent entities emerged as fully sovereign and each sovereignty tended to divert the mode of loyalty of men from universal to territorial concepts. As a result, territorial segregation constituted an underlying factor for the gradual transformation of the nature of sovereignty from universal to territorial as well as of the law from personal to territorial.

IV

Twentieth-century Islam found itself completely reconciled to the Western secular system—a system which itself had undergone radical changes from its medieval Christian background. Even Muslim thinkers who objected to the secularization of the law governing Islam's domestic affairs have accepted marked departures from the law and traditional practices governing external relations. Some called for a complete separation between religion and the state, while others advocated the establishment of an Islamic subsystem within the community of nations.[6] But no one seems to advocate the reinstatement of the traditional Islamic system of external relations. This attitude is consistent with the trend toward a world-wide community of nations that had been going on for a long time, and the active participation of Muslim states in international councils and organizations has committed Islam to the cause of peace and international security.

After World War II a few Muslim thinkers began to reflect on the enormous changes that had taken place in Islam under the impact of the West. It is not an unhealthy sign to look back at one's own achievements, whether to iron out certain mental doubts or to gather momentum for further strides. Some have regretted that Islam, having been divided into sovereign entities, has become weak; and others have taken a critical attitude toward the complete integration of Islam's public order within the larger world order. But all seem to agree that Muslim states should show a certain degree of solidarity in international councils which would enhance their prestige and serve their common interests.

Thinking along these lines has been given impetus by the rise into statehood of new Muslim states, such as Pakistan and Indonesia, to mention only two. A few Muslim leaders have called for holding Islamic conferences and forming regional pacts and alliances among Muslim states. This new trend has been called neo–Pan-Islamism, but it is not aimed at restoring Islamic unity, as was the Pan-Islamic movement of the nineteenth century, nor is it indicative of a desire to reinstate the Islamic traditional system of the conduct of external relations. It is rather a desire to cooperate as an Islamic bloc within the community of nations.

Furthermore, there are a few Muslim thinkers who, in advocating active participation in international councils, see the possibility of Islam's contributing to the development of a more stable and peaceful world order. Owing to Islam's historical contact with Christian Europe, the reconciliation between the Christian and Islamic systems might provide a precedent for the reconciliation of other rival systems. It may be asked, what are the possible contributions of Islam to an expanding world order?

First, the competition and conflict between Islam and Christendom, which lasted for centuries, demonstrated the possibility of coexistence of diverse systems and their final integration within a world-wide system, if accommodation to changing circumstances were permitted by both parties. In the emerging world community diverse systems of public order, including the Islamic, should be examined, in order to draw upon the historical experiences of nations that lived under these systems, for every matured system records the stored experience of men with the problem of how to maintain a stable public order.

Secondly, in the Islamic experience of international relations the individual was regarded as a subject of the law governing external relations, and central authorities dealt directly with the individual apart from the state. While it is true that in the past Islam recognized the individual as a subject because its system was personal—not territorial—it would seem that in a shrinking world the individual's claim to protection under the modern law of nations has become a pressing necessity. It is taken for granted that Muslims would welcome the adoption of such a principle in the modern law of nations, as reflected in their acceptance of the Declaration of Human Rights, since traditionally Islamic law recognized the individual as a subject on the international plane.

Thirdly, Islam as a way of life stresses moral principles, apart from religious doctrine, in the relations among nations. The historical experiences of Islam demonstrate this paradox: that religious doctrine as a basis for the conduct of the state promoted conflict and continuous hostilities with other nations; but religion as a sanction for moral principles prompted Muslims to take a tolerant attitude toward non-Muslims and to observe humane principles embodied in the law of war during hostilities with other nations. Thus the historical experiences of Islam, indeed the historical experiences of all mankind, demonstrate that any system of public order, on the national as well as the international plane, would become meaningless if divorced completely from moral principles.

However, the emphasis on moral principles in the intercourse among nations does not imply the reintroduction of religious doctrine in the conduct of states. The historical experiences of Christendom and Islam demonstrate that the fusion of religion—indeed any form of an ideology—with the foreign conduct of states can be very dangerous indeed. For divergent ideologies may hamper the development of relations among nations on the basis of rules and practices derived from their historical experiences and their common interest. It is unfortunate that when Islam and Christendom, after a long period of competition and rivalry, have learned the lesson of divorcing ideology from the principles and practices governing their relations, both are confronted by the rise of a new ideology which its followers seem to insist on reintroducing in the intercourse among nations. Islam's past competition and present coexistence with Christendom might well be pondered by countries that are trying to infuse ideology in the relations among nations during the crisis through which the community of nations is now passing.[7]

NOTES

1. Qur'ān, LXI, 10–13.

2. The believers may fulfill the *jihād* duty by heart, in their effort to combat the Devil and to escape his persuasion to evil; by tongue and hands in their attempt to support the right and correct the wrong; and by the sword in taking part in actual fighting and by sacrificing their "wealth and lives" (Qur'ān, LXI, 11) in the prosecution of war.

3. In Christendom the crusade was not the only *bellum justum,* but in Islam the *jihād* was the only *bellum justum.*

4. Historians divide the history of the Islamic state in accordance with ruling dynasties, beginning with the Prophet Muḥammad (d. 632), followed by the Orthodox caliphs (632–61), the Umayyad Dynasty (661–750), the 'Abbāsid Dynasty (750–1258), and a set of diverse sultanates, including the Ottoman, to the present age.

5. A third division of the Islamic world, advocating the Sunnī creed, fell under the rule of the Mughal Dynasty. The greater part of this division, comprising the Indian subcontinent, became part of the British Empire. The northern portion, leaving a small buffer territory forming modern Afghanistan, was occupied by Russia.

6. The exponent of the principle of separation between state and religion is 'Alī 'Abd al-Rāziq in his work *al-Islām wa usūl al-ḥukm* (Cairo, 1925), and the exponent of Islam as a subsystem is 'Abd al-Razzāq al-Sanhūrī in his work in *Le Califat: son évolution vers une société des nations orientales* (Paris, 1926).

7. The writer has drawn freely from his book *War and Peace in the Law of Islam* (Baltimore, 1955, 1962), and from his articles "Islam and the Modern Law of Nations," *American Journal of International Law,* Vol. 50 (1956), pp. 358–72, and "The Islamic System: Its Competition and Co-Existence with Western Systems," *Proceedings of the American Society of International Law,* 1959, pp. 49–52.

The Appeal of Communism to Islamic Peoples

By Dankwart A. Rustow

I. Communism and Islam

In September, 1920, the Bolsheviks on the eve of their victory in the Russian civil war convened a Congress of the Peoples of the East. The delegates at Baku claimed to represent a broad belt of Asian and African countries from Manchuria to Morocco, and one of their resolutions called for a *jihād* (holy war) against British imperialism. A generation later, Asian and African countries such as Egypt and Indonesia began to receive massive shipments of Soviet arms. Each time, the Russians' appeal was mostly to Islamic countries (the largest delegations at Baku were those from Turkey and Iran), and in the last decade there have been recurrent fears that one or another of these—Egypt, Syria, Iraq, Afghanistan, Indonesia, or Algeria—would be drawn into their orbit. Nonetheless, the Soviets' recent blandishments have had little more success than their earlier proclamations of Eastern solidarity: the Muslim Middle East from the Caucasus to the Pamirs remains the only area where Communist power still is confined within the borders of the old Czarist Empire.

Meanwhile, observers in both the West and the Middle East have divided sharply on the question of the intrinsic or potential relationship of Communism and Islam. One school has propounded the "bulwark of Islam theory," [1] the notion that Muslims by virtue of their religion are immune to "godless Communism." The opposite school has seen a special affinity between the two, the case being stated most succinctly by Bernard Lewis who wrote in 1953:

> Both groups profess a totalitarian doctrine, with complete and final answers to all questions on heaven and earth; the answers are different in every respect, alike only in their finality and completeness, and in the contrast they offer with the eternal questioning of Western man. Both groups offer to their members and followers the agreeable sensation of belonging to a community of believers, who are always right, as against an outer world of unbelievers, who are always wrong. Both offer an exhilarating feeling of mission, of purpose, of being engaged in a collective adventure to accelerate the historically inevitable victory of the true faith over the infidel evil-doers. The traditional Islamic division of the world into the House of Islam and the House of War, two necessarily opposed groups, of which the first has the collective obligation of perpetual struggle against the second, also has obvious parallels in the Communist view of world affairs. There again, the content of belief is utterly different, but the aggressive fanaticism of the believer

is the same. The humorist who summed up the Communist creed as "There is no God and Karl Marx is his Prophet" was laying his finger on a real affinity. The call to a Communist *Jihad,* a Holy War for the faith—a new faith, but against the selfsame Western Christian enemy—might well strike a responsive note.[2]

The debate has been singularly futile. Similar controversies could arise, and have indeed arisen, about the relationship of Communism to other world religions. Those who see a special affinity of Catholic countries for Communism will point to the postwar Communist vote in France and Italy which has consistently far exceeded that in Protestant countries. But they will draw the rejoinder that Catholicism has perceptibly strengthened Polish and Hungarian resistance to Soviet domination. Christianity, Islam, and Communism are complex bodies of doctrine which can apply to concrete historical situations in a variety of ways. The question of their interrelation is so broad as to be perforce inconclusive.[3]

I propose to approach the topic of the Communist appeal to Muslim peoples inductively rather than speculatively, and to start, not with the period of Muḥammad and the early caliphs but with that of Karl Marx. And I shall treat it primarily as a political rather than a religious or doctrinal question.

II. London to Istanbul—via Moscow

The nineteenth century was a great era of political exiles. At the time that Marx was composing *Das Kapital* in the British Museum, thousands of intellectual refugees from the domains of the Romanov czars, the Ottoman sultans, and the Qajar shahs were making their way abroad. Although some of the Iranians congregated in Calcutta and some of the Ottomans in Cairo, the most hospitable places of asylum for Russians and Middle Easterners alike were the cities of Europe—Paris, Geneva, Zurich, Brussels, and London. But their response to this same intellectual environment differed sharply. The Russians became disciples of Hegel and Feuerbach, of Blanqui and Marx, and they soon produced major radical, revolutionary, and anarchist thinkers of their own, such as Bakunin, Herzen, Kropotkin, and Lenin. The Middle Easterners came under the influence of Mazzini, Comte, Victor Hugo, Renan, and Durkheim. Whether at home or abroad, they produced thinkers concerned with nationalism and with political or religious reform, such as Midhat Pasha, Namik Kemāl, Aḥmed Rizā, Muḥammad 'Abduh, Rashīd Riḍā, Kawākibī, and Ziyā Gökalp. The divergence between Russian and Middle Eastern political thought of this period is so striking that a careful and systematic examination would seem long overdue.

In the present context only a few partial and tentative explanations can be suggested. To start with the most trivial, the Middle Easterners spoke only French, whereas the Russians spoke German as well; the Russians, moreover, began arriving in Europe toward the end of the great revolutionary era of 1789–1848, whereas most of the Middle Eastern exiles came to Europe during the stabler period of Napoleon III, Disraeli, and Bismarck. But there were deeper underlying reasons for the Russians' radicalism and the Middle Easterners' moderation. Russia had begun its westernization under Peter the Great. In the following century she established herself as a major European power, her armies crossing the Alps and the Rhine, her navy sailing into the Mediterranean. Internally, the Romanov autocracy was solidly entrenched; the Russian national character of the Empire could readily be taken for granted, though some wished to expand Russian nationalism into Pan-Slavism. Russian intellectuals participated in the major cultural currents of Europe—they wrote romantic poems and realistic novels. The contrast between the Czarist police state and the passionate social realism of a Turgenev, a Tolstoy, and a Dostoyevsky provided a compelling backdrop for radicalism and revolution.

In the Middle East, westernization began one or one-and-a-half centuries later with Selīm III and Muḥammad ʻAlī, with Maḥmūd II and the Tanẓīmāt. The political and military consequence of the early reforms was a perceptible weakening of Middle Eastern power. In the 1830's, for example, the Ottoman Empire was in danger, alternately, of becoming a Russian protectorate or a victim of Egyptian military conquest. But while the Ottoman state was far weaker than Russia, the loyalty of its exiled subjects proved far more tenacious. In contrast to the Russians who turned into sworn enemies of the Czarist regime, the Middle Eastern intellectuals never seem to have lost their sense of identification with the state. Some of them were descendants of the ruling houses, such as Muṣṭafā Fāzil Pasha of Egypt and "Prince" Sabāḥeddīn of Turkey; others had been trained as civil servants or military officers. They could cherish hopes of assuming high office as soon as a new ruler came to the throne or a new vezir to the divan. Even in exile, these men still conducted themselves like members of a political class, a governing elite: their ultimate purpose remained salvation of the Ottoman Empire. In internal Ottoman politics, the crises of 1806–07 and of 1826 had provided major contests for power between reforming, centralizing sultans and various traditional centrifugal forces—*derebeyis* and *aʻyān,* Janissaries and *ʻulamā'*. Soon, however, the nationality problem—the aspirations to independence of Greeks and Serbs, Bulgarians and Armenians, Albanians and Arabs—proved to be the Empire's fatal flaw. Quite naturally, the Ottoman exiles tended to be preoccupied with questions not of social revolution but of constitutionalism and national identity. Compared to the mass movement of the Russian Revolution of 1917, or even to that of 1905, the Young Turk "Revolution" of 1908 must be rated not as a major upheaval among social classes, but as a mere *coup d'état* within the ruling elite.

The starting point of our inquiry, then, must be that Marxism, for whatever reasons, came from the British Museum to the shores of the Bosporus and the Nile not directly but only after a long detour via the Neva and Moskva rivers. Before World War I, socialism was advocated in the Ottoman Empire only by a handful of men, most of them among the non-Muslim minorities.[4] But after the November Revolution Ottoman Turks and other Middle Easterners perforce took note of Communism, and their future attitudes were to be indelibly colored by the Russian transmission of the Communist impact.

III. Kemālists and Bolsheviks

With Russia, the Middle Easterners had had close contact for two centuries. Since the late seventeenth century, the Ottomans had been at war with the Russians at least once in every generation. It was the loss of the Crimea in 1774–83 rather than that of Hungary a hundred years earlier that launched the sultans on their efforts at military reform. In the early nineteenth century, neighboring Iran had lost vast areas in the Caucasus and in Transoxania to the advancing Czarist Empire. To the Ottomans in particular, the "Moskovs" became the legendary archenemies. Quite naturally, the revolutions of February and November of 1917 were hailed by the Ottomans as the downfall of their most formidable foe. At Brest Litovsk, Ṭal'at Pasha joined the Germans in dictating peace terms to the vanquished enemy, and in the Caucasus the disintegration of Russian armies secured for the Ottoman troops an easy conquest after four years of humiliating defeat. The Bolsheviks pursued their psychological advantage by their publication of the secret partition agreements regarding the Ottoman Empire and by their solemn repudiation of the expansionist policy of the Czar. When Muṣṭafā Kemāl Pasha in 1919 and 1920 courageously undertook to save the Empire's Anatolian rump from Allied occupation and partition, he sought diplomatic contact with the Bolsheviks who were then engaged in a life-and-death struggle against the same Western powers. The first foreign policy measure of the Ankara National Assembly in the summer of 1920 was the dispatch of a commission of inquiry to Moscow, and its first major foreign treaty was the Russian-Turkish Friendship Treaty of March 16, 1921. That same summer, several shipments of bullion and ammunition arrived to strengthen the Kemālist war effort. In the fall of 1920 a Kemālist deputy in the National Assembly sang the praises of Communism—"an ideology that has shaken the earth, that has given a new impulse to the Muslim world, that is smashing and destroying [our European enemies]—an ideology that has opened up the brightest of horizons before us. . . . The principles of Bolshevism are the scientific principles that will save the country, that will save the nation, that will save mankind." [5]

But behind this façade of enthusiastic Kemālist-Bolshevik friendship, there was much mutual suspicion, complex intrigue, and latent hostility. As early as the summer of 1920 Kemāl had warned his front commanders in a secret message that "Since the aim of Communism is unconditional subjection to Russia, the purposes of its organization [in Turkey] are diametrically opposed to our own. We must in every way stop and remove the secret Communist organizations." In view of the pending treaty negotiations, however, he added: "Naturally I do not see fit to oppose Communism and Bolshevism publicly." [6] But a few months later, even before the treaty was signed, Atatürk in a speech in the Turkish National Assembly likened Communism to a "bacillus" against which public enlightenment and governmental action would provide a suitable "remedy." [7] A few months of diplomatic contact had allowed Kemāl to recognize what many Westerners were to admit only a quarter-century later: that Bolshevism was continuing the Czar's expansionist foreign policy in a more dangerous guise.

IV. Lenin to Stalin to Khrushchev

In the forty-odd years since the Russian-Turkish Friendship Treaty, the political situation in the Islamic countries has undergone a significant transformation. In the wake of World War I, the Middle East and much of North Africa and Southern Asia were in political turmoil. The Ottoman and Qajar realms were crumbling; in Egypt, Syria, and Iraq, Arab nationalism was clashing with British and French colonialism; in the Rif, 'Abd al-Karīm was carrying on his guerrilla warfare; in India, the first stirrings of nationalist protest were led by the Muslim Khilāfat movement. By about 1921, however, the situation was largely stabilized. British rule had been re-established in Egypt, and order restored in India, new mandates had been installed throughout the Fertile Crescent, and on Russia's border Kemāl in Turkey and Rizā in Iran were consolidating their nationalist regimes. It was not until World War II and its aftermath that the situation once again came to be in flux. India and Pakistan in 1947 led the procession of newly independent Asian and later African states. With the victory of Algerian nationalism in 1962, all major Muslim countries had attained independence. The decade from 1952 to 1963 was one of revolutions in the Arab countries in which traditional monarchical and pro-Western regimes made way for popular regimes preoccupied with the question of Arab national unity. The Iranian crisis of 1953 and the Turkish one of 1960–61 revealed much latent or open political ferment in these countries as well. Although the Baghdad Pact of 1955 seemed to implement John Foster Dulles' strategy of a *cordon sanitaire* along the Near East's

Northern Tier, Iraq itself withdrew after its 1958 revolution and Pakistan was growing restless with its Western alliances. The Muslim countries, like their neighbors in Asia and Africa, were deeply involved in the active political and economic competition between the Western and Eastern blocs, and most of them clung to a policy of nonalignment.

The transformation of Soviet ideology and foreign strategy in this period has been of equally profound significance. Marx had envisaged his revolution as an almost spontaneous discharge of proletarian tensions in highly developed industrial societies, a virtually painless expropriation of the expropriators. Lenin's reinterpretation first made the doctrine relevant to societies in the early stages of industrialization. His revolutionary masses were to be led by a highly trained conspiratorial elite. Still, Lenin, like Marx, envisaged a single world-wide revolution in which the several Communist parties would freely cooperate with each other. Stalin, by contrast, achieved the complete subordination of all Communist parties under the Kremlin. At first he was preoccupied with the building of "socialism in one country." Later, the victory of Communism outside of Russia was secured (with the exception of Yugoslavia, China, and Cuba) through military occupation by Red Armies—preceded at times, as in Czechoslovakia, by an internal coup. Khrushchev, finally, substituted for Stalin's truculence and suspicion a manner at once more boisterous, suave, and seemingly more conciliatory. He also set his sights far beyond Russia's immediate periphery to countries as distant as the Congo or Cuba. Furthermore, the Russians have now been engaged for some time in a bitter intramural feud with their Chinese colleagues about the tactical application of the common Marxist-Leninist tenets of strategy.

V. The Phases of Soviet Middle Eastern Policy Since 1917

In the years after 1917, the Communists, fighting against imperialist intervention and hopeful of revolutionary successes in Germany, Hungary, and other European countries, were eager to involve the Islamic Middle East in what would become a world revolution. There was intense Communist agitation among Ottoman prisoners of war in Russia, and separate Communist parties were organized in Istanbul and in Anatolia. In 1920, Soviet troops landed in the northern Iranian province of Gilan in pursuit of White Russian contingents and proceeded to sponsor a separatist regime under Kuchik Khan. A year later, Russian and Gilani Communists were marching on Tehran where a Council of Trade Unions had recently affiliated with the Profintern. In Moscow in the summer of 1920 Enver Pasha and other Young Turk exiles founded a Pan-Islamic society with full support of the Communists. In Afghanistan, Enver's colleague, Cemāl Pasha, was reorganizing Amīr Amānullāh's army with Soviet assistance.

Far-flung and ambitious though these Communist attempts were, they did not extend to the Arab countries. Even in the northern Islamic countries on Russia's border, the year 1921 marked the failure of their revolutionary and expansionist hopes. Muṣṭafā Kemāl, after his victory over the Greeks, proceeded to outlaw all Communist organizations. Rizā Khan, at the head of his Cossack Brigade, subdued the Gilan rebels and assumed power in Tehran. Enver Pasha, frustrated by Kemāl's victories in his attempts to return to Turkey, went instead to Central Asia where he attempted to create a military alliance among the fugitive Amīr of Bukhara, the local tribesmen known as Basmajis (or "Raiders") and other anti-Bolshevik forces.[8] With Enver's battlefield death in August,

1922, and the defeat of the Basmajis, Communist rule was extended to the old Czarist border, but nowhere beyond it. (The cession of Kars and Ardahan to Turkey in 1921, indeed, somewhat diminished the territory under Russian control.)

The years from 1921 to 1939 were a period of consolidation on either side of the Russian–Middle Eastern frontier. The Soviet Union underwent the crises of the NEP, the elimination of the kulaks, the struggle for Lenin's succession, and the great purges of the 1930's. Russia periodically renewed her friendship treaties with Turkey and Iran. In the 1930's Kemālist Turkey accepted its first economic foreign aid—quite modest in amount by today's standards—so as to build up a Soviet-style textile *kombinat* at Kayseri. But local Communists and even their vague sympathizers were systematically suppressed both in Iran and Turkey; the Kemālists even demonstrated their independence of the Soviet Union by offering asylum to Trotsky on Büyükada. In Egypt, Syria, and Iraq, the small, illegal Communist movements remained quite insignificant.

That Russian expansionist ambitions had not been abandoned but merely postponed was made clear by the secret Ribbentrop-Molotov pact of 1939 which recognized "the area south of Batum and Baku in the general direction of the Persian Gulf" as the center of the Soviets' territorial aspirations. That pact also indicated the chief methods that Stalin proposed to employ in the renewed Soviet bid for penetration of the Middle East in the 1940's. Diplomatic negotiations with wartime allies, diplomatic pressure on neighbors, and military occupation beyond Russia's frontiers were to be the major tools—except that after 1941 Stalin's allies, much to his dismay, turned out to be not Nazi Germany but Britain and the United States. In 1941, British and Russian troops unceremoniously divided Iran into two occupation zones so as to secure an overland supply route to the hard-pressed Eastern front. Rizā Shah was exiled and the Allied occupation was sanctioned *ex post facto* by a tripartite agreement with the government of his son. It was here in Iran, the only area of direct contact during the war, that the Western allies received a foretaste of Russia's Cold War tactics before the end even of the hot war. Wheat shipments from Iran's major grain-producing areas in the North were diverted to the Soviet Union, while the Soviet-censored press in Tehran self-righteously blamed the resulting food shortages in the South on the rigors of capitalist occupation.[9]

But the major political offensive came immediately after the war. In the years from 1945 to 1947, Russia registered a claim to the administration of the Italian ex-colony of Libya, named "joint defense of the Straits" and territorial concessions along the Caucasus frontier as her price for renewal of the Turkish friendship treaty, set up the Azarbayjān People's Republic under the protection of Russian bayonets at Tabriz, encouraged the formation of another secessionist regime by Kurds at Māhābād, and refused to end her wartime occupation while pressing for a major concession for oil exploration throughout northern Iran. On Turkey's other flank, Communist guerrillas came close to winning the Greek civil war. In these years immediately after World War II, as earlier after World War I, Russia's main pressure was exerted upon her immediate neighbors. Only with the withdrawal of British positions of hegemony did the Communists become more active in the areas farther to the south; significantly, the Soviet Union was the first country to recognize Israel *de jure* in 1948.

It was in the Middle East rather than in Eastern Europe that the issue between Russia and the Western powers was joined, and in the face of firm counterpressure, the Soviets yielded along the entire Middle Eastern front. The Iranian case provided the occasion for the first major East-West clash in the United Nations Security Council. The Truman Doctrine threw American military and economic support behind

Greece and Turkey and prepared the admission of both countries to NATO in 1951. In Iran, the Soviets had a second opportunity in 1953, when the Communist Tudeh Party was eagerly waiting to exploit Musaddiq's bitter contest with the Shah; but the rapid restoration of the Shah by the Zāhidī coup thwarted any such hopes. The Baghdad Pact signaled the stabilization of the Cold War front along the Northern Tier.

But the year 1955 also marked the beginning of Russia's most recent strategy, which has been aptly described as one of "leapfrogging" over the West's defenses along her periphery. It has relied not on military occupation but on diplomacy; not on direct attempts to create satellite states but on appeals to neutralist and anti-Western, anticolonial sentiment; not on blunt threats but on alluring offers of arms and of economic assistance; not on a frontal push but on a more selective impact on individual countries. The high points of this Soviet strategy have been the large shipments of arms to Egypt in 1955 and the later large-scale aid for the building of the High Dam at Aswān; military aid to Syria in 1957 at a time when a Communist officer, 'Afīf al-Bizrī, served as Chief of Staff; [10] military and economic aid to Yemen; support of the early stages of Qāsim's revolution in Iraq; continuing aid of various kinds to Afghanistan; and the increasingly close cooperation between Communists and the Sukarno regime in Indonesia.

VI. Dilemmas of Communist Tactics

The alternation of aggressive and friendly Soviet policies since 1917 reflects in part the recurrent shifts between a hard "revolutionary" line of Communist strategy and a softer line of "national fronts" and support of "bourgeois nationalists" in "semicolonial countries." In addition, during each of the three activist periods (1917–21, 1945–47, 1955–58), the Soviets have faced a number of tactical dilemmas in the Middle

East. Most of these originate in the many political divisions among and within Middle Eastern countries—an intractable factor that has caused much grief to foreign-policy makers in the West as well, and, for that matter, to Middle Eastern political leaders themselves.

Take first the divisions among Middle Eastern countries and rival ethnic groups. In 1919 and 1920 the Armenian Communist movement was among the strongest in the Transcaucasus, but the Soviets' support of Armenian aspirations clearly was incompatible with their diplomatic friendship with the Kemālist Turks. In this instance, the Soviets solved the dilemma by forcing the Armenians to accept the boundary upon which Moscow and Ankara had agreed—although this concession did not earn them any lasting gratitude in Turkey. Later, early Soviet support for Israel seriously delayed the *rapprochement* with the Arabs, which in turn caused Israel to align more firmly with the West. In the late 1950's the Soviets contributed to a cooling of their relations with Nāṣir by their massive support of the Qāsim regime in Iraq. But internal political divisions turned out to be equally troublesome. In 1920, for example, the Soviets were supporting both Muṣṭafā Kemāl and Enver Pasha, who during his days of Russian exile was waiting for a chance to assume military-political leadership in Anatolia. The complex web of diplomacy and intrigue among the Narkomindel, Enver, and Kemāl in fact resembled a triangular game of double cross—and in the end both Turkish leaders turned resolutely against the Soviets. In 1957 the Communist bid for power in Syria prompted the Ba'th Party's union with Egypt.

The choice among rival factions poses a dilemma of special urgency in a middle range of involvement. When a major power is in firm control—as the Soviets were in the Transcaucasus in 1921 or the French in Syria in the interwar period—*divide et impera* serves as the classic maxim. At the other end, when a power seeks friendly relations rather than hegemony, it may cultivate a variety of associates who are themselves at odds with each other; this has been true of recent U.S. policy toward Nāṣir and King Sa'ūd, toward India and Pakistan. But when initial penetration is to be achieved, the dilemma is acute. The Soviets' natural tendency in choosing between Enver and Kemāl or Nāṣir and Qāsim was to try to back the group (a) with the best chance of success and (b) more amenable to their purposes. The two criteria may well conflict. The first clearly is the more important, but it is also harder to assess.

A related dilemma appeared in Iran in 1945–47. The question for the Russians was whether to nibble or to swallow—whether to play for firm control of Azarbayjān, antagonizing the rest of Iran, or to give up the Azarī foothold and try, through the oil concession and Tudeh Party ministers, to infiltrate the Iranian government as a whole. They gambled on the second menu but in the end went empty-mouthed altogether. Another example of this latter dilemma appeared in Algeria in the late 1940's: whether to back the nationalist insurgents or the French position on the chance that France herself, including her overseas possessions, would go Communist. Once again, the Communists played initially for the higher stakes (it was a Communist cabinet minister who ordered the suppression of the incipient rebellion) and lost. Needless to say, the transparent opportunism of the Soviet moves tends to arouse the suspicions of all the groups concerned.

VII. Cautious Responses from the Middle East

The Middle Eastern response to the Soviet impact has varied from country to country and from period to period. It has been affected by Soviet policies and by those of the West and, above all, by the geography, history, and internal politics of the Middle Eastern countries themselves.

The history of exposure to Russian expansionism in Czarist days, as we have seen, made the Turks and Iranians wary of the Communists in the 1920's. The Arabs, by contrast, had had experience with Ottoman domination and with the imperialism of Europe, not with Russia's.

> In their diplomacy, the governments of the region soon took to playing off the more remote Western Powers against those closer at hand, and major European wars were seized on as opportunities for securing greater independence. Iran long maintained a precarious sovereignty amid opposing pressures from Britain and Russia. The Arabs in the First World War invoked British help to throw off Ottoman rule, while during the Second World War men like the Mufti of Jerusalem, the Egyptian Premier Ali Mahir, and Rashid Ali, leader of the Iraq coup in 1941, were tempted to align with the Axis in order to oust the British. From their narrow perspective, many . . . Arabs . . . tend to see the present world conflict as just another dispute among two groups of European Powers. Once again the temptation is to profit from tension among the Powers to promote one's own political aspirations.[11]

But the game of playing off the distant against the nearby foreigner provides its own inexorable corrective: it brings the once-distant power into uncomfortable proximity. Just as the Arabs in the 1930's and 1940's had reason to regret Sharīf Fayṣal's close cooperation with the British after World War I, so the Arabs of the 1950's and 1960's have had occasion for second thoughts about their close association with the Communists some years before. This time, in fact, the sobering set in rather more quickly; the experience with inferior Russian equipment and standoffishness of Soviet technicians at Aswān and with their double-dealing in Iraq after 1958 sped the disillusionment. Luckily, the Arabs, being separated from Russia by Turkey and Iran, retained the freedom to act on their second thoughts—a freedom which political groups working with the Communists in Eastern Europe lost as soon as Red troops marched in. The West's recent tolerance of neutralism has helped, too. Where once Communism had the fascinating flavor of forbidden fruit, it now turns out that a little knowledge of the Bolsheviks is a most salutary thing.

The most important psychological attraction of Communism for Middle Easterners stems from the region's often unhappy experience with the West. The West has provided both the ideals of modernization, of industrialization, and of nationalism and the reality of imperial hegemony and colonial or semicolonial rule. To many citizens of the Middle East, as of other underdeveloped countries, association with the Soviets has presented itself as the ready solution for the resulting dilemma of ambivalence, as a formula by which nationalists can promote Western social and technical values at home while sharply opposing the West on the international scene.

Turkey won her victory over the West in 1919–23, and proceeded to a bold program of westernization without any sense of duress; she thereby also developed a healthy resistance to the Communist lure. The Arabs, experiencing Western colonialism in the transparent disguise of mandates, protectorates, or one-sided treaty arrangements, have been far more favorable to the Russians.

Iran is in a position somewhere between Turkey and the Arab countries in her attitudes to both Russia and the West. Iran has had ample experience with Russia over the last century and a half. The intricate maneuvers by which Premier Aḥmad Qawām in 1946–47, with the help of strong pressure from the U.S. and the U.N., frustrated all Russian designs for Azarbayjān, for oil exploration, and for Communist participation in the cabinet remains one of the most breath-taking episodes in recent diplomatic history. But Iran has even bitterer memories about Britain: the 1907 Anglo-Russian agreement in the wake of British encouragement of Iranian constitutionalism, the 1919 draft treaty that would have made the country a virtual protectorate of Britain, the protracted and fruitless negotiations with the Anglo-Iranian Oil Company. The Russians, of course, participated in the partitions of 1907 and 1941; but Iranian disappointment in the British was keener, for of the Russians nothing better was expected. Hence, the Iranian nationalist today still is likely to blame his country's ills on the sinister machinations of the British; if no connection is apparent, this only proves their deviousness and cunning. As a result, Iran long had one of the largest Communist parties of the region, thinly disguised under the Tudeh label.

The anti-Western, anticolonial attitude, however, is a wasting asset for the Communists. A decade after the withdrawal of the major Western colonial positions, the notion of colonialism as the root of all evil and backwardness is becoming somewhat threadbare. The more openly the Russians pursue their expansionist aims, the more quickly Middle Easterners are likely to abandon the so-called "salt-water fallacy"—the assumption that imperialism deserves that name only if it arrives across the high seas.

The experience of Turkey in 1920–21 and of Iraq in 1958–60, moreover, indicates that Middle Easterners are quite uninhibited in trying to beat the Communists at their own game of infiltration and of false front organizations. (That they have been less skillful at the game is, of course, another matter.) Muṣṭafā Kemāl in 1920 hit on the ingenious device of requesting some of his close associates to form an official "Turkish Communist Party." His aim became clear when the party stated, in its first circular, that "no society or committee, and no person without written authority and an official identity card [from this party] will henceforth be allowed to be active on behalf of Bolshevik or Communist principles." [12] Secretly all the top-ranking military commanders were to sit on the party's central committee, it being understood that Communist agitation in the army would be strictly confined to the highest ranks. The Russians themselves were hardly deceived by this ruse. Zinoviev denounced the Ankara group as "toys" and a Soviet expert on Turkey called them "usurpers and hypocrites, veritable wolves in sheep's clothing." [13] A very similar maneuver was undertaken by Qāsim, who soon after the 1958 revolution closed all parties including the Communists and forbade the bearing of arms especially by the Communist militias. When political parties once again were permitted, the *bona fide* Communists saw their application rejected since the name "Iraqi Communist Party" had been pre-empted by a group of Qāsim's own followers. When they reapplied under a new name, they were again turned down on the ground that their program was essentially the same as that of the officially licensed group. Once again, Moscow was not deceived, but internal Communist organization suffered some disarray. Nāṣir similarly has dismayed the Soviets by cheerfully accepting Soviet aid while resolutely suppressing Communist organization in his country.

Next to the mixed and often bitter memory of relations with the West, the most important factor enhancing the appeal of Communism is the frustrations of Middle Eastern domestic politics, such as the long unfulfilled hopes for unity among the Arabs and the pent-up demand for social reform in Iran. The difficulties of social and political reconstruction in Algeria, the internal turmoil that may result from a fall of the monarchic regimes in Saudi Arabia, in Jordan, and in Libya may provide new opportunities for Communist propaganda and political maneuver. Even in Turkey, the social tensions laid bare by the crisis of 1960–61 have given a new impetus among certain intellectual circles to a brand of socialism that comes perilously close to fellow-traveling Communism.[14] Yet, by and large, the Middle Eastern experience of the last decade confirms that the popular political leaders of the region are nationalists dedicated to strengthening their own power position and to enhancing the political stature of their countries among the other nations of the world. The Russian retreat from Azarbayjān in 1946–47 remains the only occasion when Soviet control was "rolled back." Above all, the lessons of recent Middle Eastern history should do much to dispel the misconception long popular in the West of the Kremlin's diabolic infallibility.

NOTES

1. In the apt phrase of Walter Z. Laqueur, a sharp critic of that theory. See his *Communism and Nationalism in the Middle East* (2d ed.; New York, 1957), pp. 5 ff.

2. "Communism and Islam," *The Middle East in Transition,* ed. Walter Z. Laqueur (New York, 1958), pp. 302 f.

3. For a critical review of the controversy between the "Two opposing views of Islam's relationship to communism . . . neither of them valid" and a perceptive statement of the true relationship, see Manfred Halpern, *The Politics of Social Change in the Middle East and North Africa* (Princeton, 1963), pp. 156–95; the quotation is at the beginning of the chapter.

4. See Louise Nalbandian, *The Armenian Revolutionary Movement* (Berkeley and Los Angeles, 1963), pp. 104 ff., on the Social Democrat Hunchakian Party, which was formed in 1890 and adopted this name in 1909; and Tarik Z. Tunaya, *Türkiyede Siyasî Partiler* (Istanbul, 1952), pp. 303 ff., on socialist organization in Salonica and in the Ottoman parliament after 1908.

5. Muhīddīn Bahā (Pars), *Türkiye Büyük Millet Meclisi Zabit Ceridesi,* November 22, 1920.

6. Quoted in Ali Fuat Cebesoy, *Millî Mücadele Hatiralari* (Istanbul, 1953), pp. 474 f.

7. *Atatürk'ün Söylev ve Demeçleri* (Ankara, 1945–54), Vol. 1, pp. 131 f. For the most careful account of Bolshevik-Kemālist relations, see Gotthard Jäschke, "Le Rôle du communisme dans les relations russo-turques de 1919 à 1922," *Orient,* Vol. 7 (1963), pp. 31–44.

8. On Enver's career in exile see my article "Enwer Pāshā," *Encyclopaedia of Islam* (new ed., 1963), Vol. 2, pp. 698–702.

9. See George Lenczowski, *Russia and the West in Iran* (Ithaca, 1949).

10. See Gordon Torrey, "The Role of the Military in Society and Government in Syria and the Formation of the U.A.R.," *The Military in the Middle East,* ed. Sydney N. Fisher (Columbus, Ohio, 1963), p. 66.

11. Quoted from my article "Defense of the Near East," *Foreign Affairs,* Vol. 34 (January, 1956), pp. 278–79.

12. Cebesoy, *op. cit.,* p. 508.

13. Quoted by Laqueur, *Communism and Nationalism,* p. 208. Laqueur, who relies entirely on Russian and European sources, is clearly ignorant of the details on the Turkish side; he confesses that "The situation on the whole" seems to him "extremely muddled" (*ibid.*). Caught in this muddle, he evidently underestimates the striking accuracy of the Soviet charges.

14. See my article "Turkey's Second Try at Democracy," *Yale Review,* Vol. 52 (Summer, 1963), pp. 518–38.

Islam and Neutralism

By Fayez A. Sayegh

It is safe to assume, I suppose, that the selection of "Islam and International Relations" as the theme of this volume of essays implies that there is some significant and direct connection between the profession of Islam and the conduct of international relations by Muslim statesmen. If this assumption is correct, then I fear that my contribution will be an heretical one.

For I shall submit that—at least with respect to "neutralism," which is a major foreign-policy problem for Muslim leaders, and therefore a suitable test case—Islam has had little, if any, noticeable influence upon the reasoning, planning, decision-making, or expression of Muslim policy-makers, neutralist and counterneutralist alike. Three independent lines of investigation lead to this conclusion, jointly suggesting the irrelevance of Islam to neutralism.

I

Let us begin with the obvious.

In the post-World War II era—characterized *inter alia* by accelerated decolonization in Asia and Africa; by the emergence of many new states, including twenty-five Muslim states, in those two continents; and by the rise of the Cold War and of neutralism—many leaders of predominantly Muslim countries have chosen to follow a neutralist course in world affairs; some have been in the vanguard of the neutralist movement. But many other Muslim leaders have chosen counterneutralist policies, aligning their countries, eagerly or without much enthusiasm, with Western powers or power blocs. At the same time, many non-Muslim countries have pursued a policy of neutralism in the Cold War. Thus, not all Muslim countries are neutralist, nor are all neutralist countries Muslim.

This phenomenon suggests *prima facie* that there is no apparent correlation between the Muslim character of a society and its neutralist (or counterneutralist) orientation.

It is possible to determine with satisfactory precision the distribution of the countries concerned among the three categories of "Muslim neutralist," "Muslim non-neutralist," and "non-Muslim neutralist." For it is fairly easy to identify those countries that may be described as Muslim and, apart from one or two borderline cases, those that may qualify as neutralist.

If we adopt as a working definition the statement that a *Muslim country* is one in which a majority of the population professes Islam, we find that there are at present twenty-five Muslim sovereign states technically competent to formulate their own foreign policies. Twelve of these are Arab, members of the League of Arab States: Algeria, Libya, Morocco, the Sudan, Tunisia, and the United Arab Republic in North Africa; and Iraq, Jordan, Kuwait, Saudi Arabia, Syria, and Yemen in Western Asia.[1] In all these Arab states, Islam is the religion of the predominant majority. Of the remaining thirteen independent Muslim states, seven lie in Africa (Chad, Guinea, Mali, Mauritania, Niger, Senegal, and Somalia) and six in Asia (Afghanistan, Indonesia, Iran, Malaya, Pakistan, and Turkey). Islam is the religion of the predominant majority in the six Asian countries and in two of the African countries (namely, Mauritania and Somalia), and of more than half but no more than three-quarters of the population of Chad, Guinea, Mali, Niger, and Senegal.

As for identifying *neutralist countries*, perhaps the least arbitrary of several possible criteria we might apply is the consensus of generally recognized neutralist states, signified by the standards agreed upon in the Preparatory Meeting for the Conference of the Uncommitted Countries, which was held in Cairo from June 5 to 12, 1961. According to its official communiqué of June 12, 1961, the Cairo meeting "discussed the problem of sending invitations to the [Belgrade] Conference, and agreed on the criterium which should be applied in regard to these invitations." [2] Although the communiqué did not spell out the criterion upon which the twenty participating governments agreed, a semiofficial Cairo periodical authoritatively revealed that the conferees "made clear that 'no country can be called a non-aligned power merely because it has given its vote in international conferences on the side of neutralist powers.' " [3] The determining factors were *neutralist conduct* and *neutralist posture.* In order to qualify for admission, governments "should exercise in practical terms a neutralist policy"—it being generally accepted that the quintessence of such policy is that "states should decide their own policies in their official capitals without regard to contending world camps." [4] It was on the basis of their appraisal of the political record and attitudes of individual governments in practice, and not merely on the basis of *professed* neutralism or *formal* nonalignment, that the Cairo conferees drew up their list of invitees for the Belgrade summit neutralist conference. If professions alone, or formal status alone, had been the guiding principle, some of the countries excluded from the list would have been included and some of the invitations would have been unjustified.

The governments that, in the collective judgment of generally recognized neutralists, were considered authentically neutralist in mid-1961 were those that were invited to, and that participated in, the Conference of Heads of State or Government of Non-Aligned Countries held in Belgrade from September 1 to 6, 1961. They were the governments of the following twenty-five countries: [5]

- Afghanistan
- Algeria (Provisional Government)
- Burma
- Cambodia
- Ceylon
- Congo (Léopoldville)
- Cuba
- Cyprus
- Ethiopia
- Ghana
- Guinea
- India
- Indonesia
- Iraq
- Lebanon
- Mali
- Morocco
- Nepal
- Saudi Arabia
- Somalia
- Sudan
- Tunisia
- United Arab Republic (Egypt and Syria)
- Yemen
- Yugoslavia

Some changes have overtaken the composition of the neutralist family since September, 1961, however. It is highly probable that, if another summit neutralist conference were to be held today, the invitation list would reflect those changes, omitting some names that appeared on the Belgrade roster and adding some new names. The following changes must therefore be taken into account:

1. *Algeria,* which was represented at Belgrade by the Prime Minister of its Provisional Government, has in the meantime attained its independence. Its duly instituted government has pursued a policy of forthright neutralism, by Cairo-Belgrade standards.

2. *Cuba,* which even in 1961 stood perilously close to the outer edge of neutralism, has since then moved beyond the border line into the zone of alignment with the Soviet bloc. It is doubtful that a majority of neutralist governments would today accept Cuba as a neutralist country.

3. *Saudi Arabia,* whose admission to the Belgrade conference in 1961 was far from noncontroversial, may have completely disqualified itself in the meantime. I doubt very strongly that Saudi Arabia would today command the confidence of a majority of neutralist countries as a *bona fide* member of the community of neutralists.

4. *The United Arab Republic* consisted, during the Cairo and Belgrade conferences, of the southern and northern regions, Egypt and Syria. But on September 28, 1961, Syria seceded from the union, and promptly regained its pre-1958 status as an independent state. Between the fall of 1961 and the winter of 1963, the foreign policy (as well as the regional and domestic policies) of Syria was ambivalent, to say the least. Since the revolution of March 8, 1963, however, the new Syrian government has re-emphasized the country's neutralist role in world affairs. Syria would, without doubt, occupy an independent place in a gathering of neutralist states today.

5. *Kuwait,* which became independent one week after the Cairo Preparatory Meeting adjourned, was immediately confronted by the crisis resulting from the claims advanced by the late Premier Qāsim of Iraq. That crisis, by leading to the invocation of the Anglo-Kuwaiti Agreement of June 19, 1961,

and the entry of British forces into Kuwait, dramatized both the dependence and the alignment of the new state. At that point, neither the Kuwaiti Government nor the neutralist community was in a mood to consider the subject of Kuwait's participation in Belgrade. In the two years that have elapsed since June, 1961, however, many factors in the Kuwaiti situation have changed. The independence of Kuwait has been widely recognized. The country has been admitted to the United Nations, as the 111th member. British forces have been withdrawn from Kuwaiti territory. Since February 8, 1963, a new regime has ruled in Baghdad; cordial visits have been exchanged between Iraqi and Kuwaiti leaders; and the dispute, though not formally resolved, is in abeyance. Thus most of the *external* causes that obtained in 1961 and counseled against the admission of Kuwait to the neutralist community have now been eliminated. More significantly, a re-examination of its foreign policy has been in the making *within* Kuwait, largely at the initiative of the new National Assembly. Accordingly, the government formally committed itself to a policy of "positive neutrality and nonalignment," in the statement made by the Minister of Foreign Affairs upon the admission of his country to membership in the United Nations on May 14, 1963, and in the policy statement made by him before (and endorsed by) the National Assembly on June 8, 1963.

If the representatives of governments generally recognized as neutralist were to reassemble now, in mid-1963, in order to make preparations for a new neutralist conference, taking into account such relevant changes in the status and policies of various states as have occurred since mid-1961, they would certainly reconfirm the invitation to *Algeria* and extend a separate invitation to *Syria;* they would probably exclude *Cuba;* and they would possibly drop *Saudi Arabia* from, and add *Kuwait* to, the revised invitation list.

Comparing the up-to-date list of twenty-five neutralist

states (Muslim and non-Muslim) with the list of twenty-five independent Muslim states (neutralist and non-neutralist), we find that fourteen countries appear on both lists (being both Muslim and neutralist), while eleven appear on each of the two lists separately (being either Muslim non-neutralists or non-Muslim neutralists). (See Table I.)

TABLE I

DISTRIBUTION OF MUSLIM AND/OR NEUTRALIST COUNTRIES

	Muslim Neutralist	*Muslim Non-Neutralist*	*Non-Muslim Neutralist*
ARAB (MEMBERS OF THE LEAGUE OF ARAB STATES)	1. Algeria 2. Iraq 3. Kuwait 4. Morocco 5. Sudan 6. Syria 7. Tunisia 8. United Arab Republic (Egypt) 9. Yemen	1. Jordan 2. Libya 3. Saudi Arabia	1. Lebanon
NON-ARAB: ASIAN	10. Afghanistan 11. Indonesia	4. Iran 5. Malaya 6. Pakistan 7. Turkey	2. Burma 3. Cambodia 4. Ceylon 5. India 6. Nepal
NON-ARAB: AFRICAN	12. Guinea 13. Mali 14. Somalia	8. Chad 9. Mauritania 10. Niger 11. Senegal	7. Congo 8. Ethiopia 9. Ghana
NON-ARAB: OTHER			10. Cyprus 11. Yugoslavia

The distribution of the countries concerned—the Muslim and/or neutralist countries—into the three distinct categories shown in Table I reveals a clear lack of correlation between Islam and neutralism, as far as the actual practice of statesmanship by Muslim leaders is concerned. Islam appears to be neither a necessary cause for, nor an impediment to, neutralism; otherwise, either all or none of the Muslim states would be neutral. Neutralism appears to be neither a distinctive feature of Muslim societies (else it would be confined to them) nor an essential element in, and therefore necessary concomitant of, Islam (else it would be espoused by all Muslim states), nor yet incompatible with Islam (as the performance of more than half of Islamdom demonstrates). The two circles, Islam and neutralism, overlap—but only in a limited segment: neutralism at one and the same time overflows the bounds of, and cuts across, the world of Islam.

This is the testimony of the facts at hand, the conclusion of our first empirical investigation into the actual relation between Islam and neutralism in the world of today. It is important that we draw the valid inference from the data—neither more nor less. In themselves, the facts marshaled thus far establish a negative conclusion—a conclusion of some importance but of limited scope. And we must guard as vigilantly against reading too much into the testimony of the phenomena as against ignoring the evidence.

The facts argue conclusively against the postulation of a simple and direct relationship between the profession of Islam and the espousal of neutralism (or counterneutralism).

So much the evidence does establish. But the possibility of other relations—perhaps more subtle, or more complex—between the profession of Islam and the espousal or rejection of neutralism is not precluded by the evidence at hand.

May it not be hypothesized that the decision-makers of the eleven Muslim governments that have chosen to align themselves with Cold War parties, and the policy-makers of the fourteen Muslim governments that have chosen nonalignment, are unequally attached to their common faith? Two possibilities suggest themselves. First, may it not be that one group is more devoutly, more authentically, or more intelligently Muslim than the other? Second, may it not be that one group is committed to the proposition that Islam has some direct bearing on international relations and national policy, while the other group is consciously or unconsciously secular? If either explanation is sound, have we not grossly erred, in our analysis thus far, in equating all Muslim states, *qua* Muslim, and in ignoring such diversity as may exist in the quality and kind of Islam practiced by Muslim policy-makers?

When it comes to judging the degree or the quality of the religious devotion of different Muslim leaders, I must plead incompetence. I do not feel qualified to judge whether the non-neutralist Shah of Iran is more, or less, devout than the neutralist King of Afghanistan, or which of the two soldier-statesmen who preside over the destinies of non-neutralist Pakistan and neutralist Sudan is the "better Muslim."

As for the potentially more relevant question—namely, whether or not the two groups of rulers entertain different concepts of the role of Islam in national and international affairs, which may account for their pursuit of opposite foreign policies—the evidence decidedly points to a negative answer. For the clear-cut division of Muslim rulers into neutralists and non-neutralists does not neatly correspond to their division into secularists and nonsecularists. Nor does there appear to be any correlation between "secularism" on the domestic level and "secularism" on the international level, even as far as the same person is concerned. Kings Ḥasan of Morocco and Idrīs of Libya are separated in foreign policy by the fence that divides neutralists from non-neutralists; but they are closer to one another in their vision of Islamic polity than is King Ḥasan to his neighbors and fellow-neutralists,

President Bourguiba (Bū-Raqībah) and Premier Ben Bella (bin-Ballā), or than is the King of Libya to the antineutralist but secularist leaders of Turkey. And some Muslim leaders, both secularist and nonsecularist, have passed from neutralism to non-neutralism, or vice versa, at times imperceptibly and at other times abruptly, in a manner that can only suggest that their positions with respect to secularism have had little or no effect upon their foreign policy choices. Thus, Bourguiba's secularism has had as little to do with his pre-Bizerte opposition to neutralism as with his post-Bizerte dramatic conversion to neutralism. And Sa'ūd's special brand of orthodoxy appears to have had little influence on his rhythmic oscillation between part-time flirtation with neutralism (as in 1955–56; and again in 1961, when he participated by proxy in the Belgrade conference) and indirect alignment (as in 1957–58, and since 1961).

Differences may exist in the degree of attachment of Muslim leaders to their faith and in their concepts of the role of Islam in public affairs. But these differences do not explain the advocacy of neutralism by some Muslim governments and its rejection by others. Nor do they aid us in our search for a meaningful relation between Islam and neutralism (or antineutralism).

Perhaps the apparent lack of correlation between Islam and neutralism (or antineutralism) may be accounted for in terms of another hypothesis. Rather than inferring that Islam is irrelevant to neutralism, may we not assume that the adoption of neutralism by some Muslim leaders and the opposition of others to neutralism were caused by differing interpretations of the teachings of Islam? May it not be the diversity in the interpretation and application of Islam, rather than the indifference of Islam to foreign policy, that has led to the adoption of divergent foreign policies by Muslim states? May it be that both neutralist and non-neutralist Muslims are equally inspired by what they consider to be authentic Islamic principles, and that they all choose and act as faithful Muslims though they choose and act in manifestly different ways? May we not therefore attribute the patent diversity of national orientations in the world of Islam neither to the irrelevance of Islam as such to foreign policy, nor to the indifference of some Muslim statesmen to their faith, but rather to the capacity of Islam for varying interpretations in the area of international relations and to Islam's ability to inspire diverse foreign policies?

To suggest an answer to these questions, the data we have surveyed thus far cannot give us much help. We must embark on a new process of investigation. We must search the thoughts and utterances of Muslim statesmen for the light that has eluded us while we have focused on the outward manifestations of their inner being.

Let us then proceed to explore the *apologias* of Muslim leaders, neutralist and antineutralist, seeking there some idea about the influence that Islam may have exerted upon the policy choice of its adherents—direct or indirect, forceful or feeble, open or hidden, and conscious or unconscious as that influence may have been.

II

I must confess that I have not read every book, article, statement, and interview of every contemporary Muslim statesman. But I think that I have studied, over the years, a fairly representative cross-section of the voluminous literature in question.

I must confess also that the results of my search have been disappointing. I have no harvest of quotations to show for my search. I can produce no catalogue of influences exercised by Islam upon the statesmanship and policy-making processes of contemporary Muslim leaders in world affairs. For I have found neither indications nor admissions of such influence, neither explicit references nor allusions.

This is of course disappointing. But it is also astonishing. For Muslim statesmen and their numerous spokesmen and apologists have not been reluctant, as a rule, to invoke Islam in justification of their choices of *national* policies—monarchism or republicanism, private enterprise or socialism, revolution or quiescence, and nationalism or supranational bonds. But they have been uncharacteristically uncommunicative regarding the Islamic rationale of their *foreign* policies. Though generally anxious to proclaim the Islamic inspiration of their decisions, and resourceful in finding Islamic vindication for the policy choices they make with respect to *national* affairs, they become strangely reticent when it comes to expounding the real or alleged Islamic grounds for their chosen positions in *international* affairs. Their customary eagerness to display the imprimatur of Islam is suddenly suppressed as soon as they turn to foreign policy.

This phenomenon would not be very astonishing, though it would be unusual, if there were Muslim consensus on foreign policy orientation. The resultant noncontroversial status of neutralism (or counterneutralism) might then account to some extent for the general disinclination to involve the faith in the advocacy of a policy already widely approved by the faithful or in the attack upon a policy already widely discredited. But such has not been the situation. The opposite has been the case. The advent of neutralism has rocked the Muslim world. It has divided contemporary Muslim leaders and peoples more sharply than any other public issue. It has stirred a passionate debate, and has occasioned the exchange of vitriolic criticism and vituperation over the air waves and in the press for years. And yet it has seldom been in the name of Islam that "traitors" have been violently denounced for their advocacy of alignment or neutralism. And seldom has it been in terms of Islamic values or principles that the merits of neutralism or alignment have been rationally expounded and calmly pleaded for or expostulated against, on rarer occasions when gentle suasion has supplanted threat, calumny, and condemnation. On the contrary, discussions of foreign policy, unlike discussions of internal policy, have entirely ignored Islam, and have been conducted exclusively in terms of national interest and/or general humanistic values.

It is not only the banishment of an otherwise ubiquitous Islam from Muslim discussions of foreign policy that is astonishing; what is equally astonishing is the replacement of Islam by extraneous principles and values. The marks of Islam upon the thought processes and expressions of Muslim leaders, in matters relating to internal affairs and national institutions, are pervasive and unmistakable; but, in matters pertaining to international affairs in general and neutralism in particular, the reasoning of the contemporary generation of Muslim leaders is indistinguishable from that of non-Muslims. Nāṣir, Nehru, Nkrumah—do they not seem to speak the same language and to draw inspiration from the same public philosophy when they discourse on neutralism and the Cold War, much in the way that Jamālī and Romulo seemed to be echoing a common tradition of thought and faith whenever they pleaded for alignment?

To put it differently: Even casual acquaintance with the writings and sayings of Muslim leaders on internal national affairs yields some knowledge about their understanding of the sociopolitical tenets of Islam; whereas thorough and careful study of the utterances of Muslim leaders on foreign policy, in pursuit of enlightenment about their interpretation of the teachings of Islam regarding current international problems, is singularly unrewarding and uninstructive.

The findings of our second process of investigation are as negative as the conclusions of our first line of inquiry. The lack of discernible correlation between Islam and neutralism (or counterneutralism), suggested by our earlier examination of the actual choices made by Muslim policy-makers, is likewise intimated by our futile search for indicators of Islamic influence in the policy- and decision-making processes of Muslim statesmanship. Neither inquiry yields direct evidence.

One is strongly tempted to draw, from such lack of evidence, a negative inference relating to the substance of the case. But this temptation should be resisted, for lack of evidence of influence is not tantamount to evidence of lack of influence.

We must look elsewhere—either for some link between Islam and foreign-policy orientation that has so far remained hidden or disguised; or for clear proof of irrelevance.

III

Thus far, we have spoken of neutralism without qualification, as though it were simple, uniform, and undifferentiated. But neutralism manifests wide diversity. Perhaps the evidence for which we have searched in vain has remained unexposed because we have failed to take into account the diversity of neutralism.

Is there a type of neutralism that has shown itself more appealing to Muslims than other types, or more attractive to Muslims than to non-Muslims? Do the actual choices of Muslim statesmen display a special proneness to the adoption of some forms of neutralism and the avoidance of others?

If a comparison of the choices of Muslim and non-Muslim neutralists among the various forms of neutralism reveals some constant pattern or some recurring preference, or some affinity between Muslim statesmanship and some specific types of neutralism, then the discovery of such affinity is likely to aid us in our inquiry into the relevance of Islam as such to neutralism. It may at least provide a welcome clue.

I view neutralism as a genus, under which several species are subsumed.[6]

The generic nature of neutralism may be defined as objection to the Cold War, resistance to its demands, aversion to involvement in its antagonisms, and eschewal of participation in its systems of alliances and treaty organizations.

Despite their common opposition to the Cold War, however, neutralists differ from one another in several important respects. For our present purposes, the principal bases of differentiation may be reduced to two: "why?" and "how?"; or motivation and orientation; or the different roads followed by neutralists on their separate journeys toward neutralism, and the manifold ways in which they express their common objection to the Cold War.

At the risk of oversimplification, we may group the reasons for the opposition of neutralists to the Cold War under three "categories of motivation," which may be labeled "doctrinaire," "ideological," and "nationalist-pragmatic."

Doctrinaire neutralists oppose the Cold War *per se*. They do so out of dedication to the ideal of international amity and to the principle of peaceful settlement of international disputes; and out of apprehension lest the consolidation and expansion of antagonistic power systems, confronting each other in mutual fear and suspicion across a rising fence of hostility, exacerbate existing tensions and precipitate the ruinous collision.

Appalled by the prevailing "climate of war," they strive to foster a "climate of peace" instead. They retort to the Cold War design of "expansive engagement" by a neutralist diplomacy of "disengagement."

Ideological neutralists question the postulated antithesis between the contending ideologies of the Cold War, and repudiate the claim of either doctrine to absoluteness and universal validity. They also challenge the thesis that ideological differences must translate themselves into political discord and military struggle. They abhor the attempts to dichotomize the world into two monolithic ideological camps, and deplore the striving of each bloc to win recruits for its crusade among members of the other bloc or among uncommitted peoples. They condemn such "proselytism" regardless of the form it takes—whether cajolery or pressure, whether overt interference or indirect subversion. They insist upon exercising their right to adopt the social, economic, and political system of their choice, and on safeguarding their freedom of selection against interference from either side.

They retort to the ideological Cold War by proclaiming the principle of "peaceful coexistence," which they apply to their own relations with both camps and which they hope to see applied also in the relations between the rival camps. Another part of their positive answer to the ideological Cold War is their attempt to advance an alternative to the contending ideologies: an independent, original alternative; or a synthesis of the antithetical systems; or, as is more often the case, an eclectic amalgam of diverse ingredients borrowed from both. In a more fanciful vein, some ideological neutralists envision their home-grown system as a potential substitute for the rival systems of East and West and as a basis for transcendence by all mankind of the ideological either/or of the Cold War.

Unlike their doctrinaire and ideological counterparts, *pragmatic neutralists* approach the Cold War without preconceived ideas about international conflict in general and without benefit of an ideological alternative. If they refuse to participate in the Cold War, it is because they deem the avoidance of entanglement to be in their nations' best interest. More often than not, their opposition is directed not at the Cold War system as such but at the policies or designs of one power bloc (or of both blocs) or of particular powers in either or both camps. Their choices are prompted primarily by practical and realistic considerations of national self-interest; and their attitudes reflect the historical, political, or economic verities of their national situation.

Neutralists in general stand out as the "objectors to the Cold War." The *doctrinaire* among them, however, are the "conscientious objectors" *par excellence. Ideological* neutralists, who cherish their nonidentification with the cause of either rival, refuse to serve flags that do not represent their own persuasion; and, in addition, they take exception to the proposition that difference in beliefs is a valid cause for enmity. They are like someone who objects to "wars of religion" in principle, and who also refuses to be drafted into participation in a religious war between two faiths which are equally remote from his own convictions. The *nationalist-pragmatic* neutralist chooses not to get into the fray because he refuses to rally behind an alien flag; he disdains the role of a mercenary and spurns enlisting in a "foreign legion" to fight the battles of others.

It goes without saying that the three causes of neutralism are not mutually preclusive. A neutralist may oppose the Cold War for two, or even for all three, of these reasons. It is in fact unrealistic not to assume that all neutralists (and, for that matter, all statesmen, regardless of their political complexion) are to some extent nationalistic and pragmatic in their approach to foreign affairs; and, while some may have no other motivation for their neutralism, some may be prompted additionally by doctrinaire concepts, some by ideological considerations, and some by both factors.

Whatever the reasons for his objection to the Cold War, however, a neutralist may express his neutralism in one (or more) of four ways. These constitute the "modalities of orientation" of neutralism, and may be designated "passive," "negative," "positive," and "messianic."

Passive neutralism evinces indifference to, and disinterest in, the Cold War as a whole. It is basically an isolationist attitude, which most countries sooner or later outgrow.

Negative neutralism, or nonalignment, signifies the refusal of a government to participate, directly or indirectly, in the power arrangements devised by either principal in the East-West conflict or to be entangled in their animosities. As such, it is the condition *sine qua non* of neutralism.

Nonalignment is prompted by the determination of a nation to safeguard its independence of judgment and policy-making and to abstain from committing itself in advance to policies formulated by others. Hence the special appeal of nonalignment to recently liberated nations, highly sensitive as they are to any real or seeming infringement on their sovereignty and averse to abdicating the prerogative of independent policy-making.

Positive neutralism goes one step beyond nonalignment. It arises when a nation, while scrupulously maintaining its independence of both power blocs, proceeds nevertheless to establish and expand economic, cultural, and other forms of normal relations with other powers, without regard to the ideological complexion of their regimes or to their positions in the Cold War system. Positive neutralism thus signifies the eager cultivation by a neutralist government of peaceful and useful relations with countries lying on both sides of the Cold War fence, to the extent to which this can be accomplished without engendering undue dependence upon either bloc (such as might produce virtual *de facto* alignment) and without requiring politicomilitary association with, or involvement in, the Cold War designs of either bloc.

If passive neutralism reflects disinterest in, and negative neutralism means rejection of the demands of, the Cold War, positive neutralism represents transcendence of the confining limits imposed by Cold War arrangements upon normal intercourse among nations; it represents a nation's exercises in leapfrogging, bypassing, or circumventing the barriers of Cold War alliances while also avoiding entanglement in their web. The fourth (or messianic) variety of neutralism, however, confronts the Cold War, looks it in the face, as it were, and tries to do something curative about its disputes and tensions.

Messianic neutralism signifies the endeavor of nonpartisan neutralists to help mankind navigate the mine field of Cold War animosities on its march toward survival and orderly peace. Its task is therefore twofold: to defuse specific disputes now, and to help lay the foundations for a less fragile future world order. Its immediate and short-range objective, of contributing to the reduction of Cold War tensions and to the peaceful resolution of particular interbloc problems, it seeks to attain by means of mediation, conciliation, or other methods of peacemaking, both within and outside the United Nations. But its long-range diplomacy aims at preparing the ground for the erection of an international system in which collaboration among nations in peace supplants their constant preparation for war, and in which pluralism supplants the attempted thorough bipolarization of mankind that is the strategy objective of Cold War partisans. For the ultimate ideal is a pluralistic world of sovereign nations, free of the polarization generated by the existence of mutually hostile, monolithic alliances. As a means for the attainment of this goal, messianic neutralism endeavors to strengthen and universalize the United Nations, reinforce its peacekeeping and peacemaking abilities, and render it the effective instrument of orderly and just peace that the Charter intended it to be.

Like the three modalities of neutralist motivation, the four modalities of neutralist orientation are not mutually preclusive. Passive and negative neutralism may, and often do, go together; negative neutralism is far from incompatible with its positive counterpart; and messianic neutralism, while it cannot coexist with passive neutralism, may harmoniously exist side by side with negative and positive neutralism.

Moreover, these varieties of neutralist orientation often make their appearance in a nation's history as successive phases in a process of evolution.

Finally, some types of motivation have special affinity for some forms of orientation. The nationalist-pragmatic approach to the Cold War lends itself more readily to the development of passive-negative or of negative-positive neutralism, whereas the ideological-doctrinaire approaches are specially conducive to messianic activism in neutralist diplomacy.

Now, if we examine the pattern of distribution of neutralist countries, Muslim and non-Muslim, among the various categories of neutralism, we may conceivably find a link—perhaps an unconscious link—between faith and policy.

The actual distribution of Muslim and non-Muslim neutralists into the three categories of motivation and the four categories of orientation is shown in Table II. It is clear from the table that there is no special pattern that distinguishes the choices of Muslim neutralists. In fact, such general tendencies as are manifested in the choices of Muslim leaders serve only to demonstrate the irrelevance of Islam. For, first, the patterns of preferences of the two groups of neutralists, Muslim and non-Muslim, are more or less similar. Second, the kinds of neutralism most frequently favored by Muslim leaders (namely, nationalist-pragmatic motivation and negative or negative-positive orientation) are those that provide the smallest opportunity for the influence of Islam (or of any other religious tradition) to be felt. And, third, the types of neutralist motivation and orientation in which values or principles inspired by religion of any kind (and *a fortiori* by Islam) are capable of expressing themselves (namely, doctrinaire or ideological motivation, and passive or messianic orientation) are either (a) shunned by Muslim neutralists, as in the case of the majority, or (b) adopted—but by a few, belatedly, and without reference to Islam.

The very negation that was hinted at by the findings of our two earlier investigations, but for which no direct evi-

CLASSIFICATION OF NEUTRALIST GOVERNMENTS (MUSLIM AND NON-MUSLIM) ACCORDING TO TYPES OF MOTIVATION AND ORIENTATION

COUNTRY		TYPE OF MOTIVATION			TYPE OF ORIENTATION			
		Doctrinaire	*Ideological (Socialist)*	*Nationalist-Pragmatic*	*Passive*	*Negative (Nonalignment)*	*Positive*	*Messianic*
MUSLIM								
Arab	1. Algeria		x	x		x	x	
	2. Iraq	x?	x	x		x	x	x?
	3. Kuwait			x	x?	x?		
	4. Morocco			x		x	x	
	5. Sudan			x		x	x	
	6. Syria	x?	x	x		x	x	x?
	7. Tunisia		x?	x		x	x?	
	8. U.A.R. (Egypt)	x	x	x		x	x	x
	9. Yemen			x	x?	x	x	
Asian	10. Afghanistan			x	x?	x	x	
	11. Indonesia	x	x	x		x	x	x
African	12. Guinea	x?	x	x		x	x	x
	13. Mali	x?	x	x		x	x	x
	14. Somalia			x		x	x	
NON-MUSLIM								
Asian	1. Burma	x	x	x		x	x	x
	2. Cambodia		x	x		x	x	
	3. Ceylon	x?	x?	x		x	x	x?
	4. India	x	x	x		x	x	x
	5. Lebanon			x		x	x?	
	6. Nepal			x	x?	x		
African	7. Congo			x	x?	x		
	8. Ethiopia			x		x	x	
	9. Ghana	x	x	x		x	x	x
Other	10. Cyprus			x		x	x	
	11. Yugoslavia	x	x?	x		x	x	x

dence was discovered, is corroborated by some direct evidence yielded by our present inquiry.

Let us look first at the categories of motivation.

It is reasonable to expect that when a religion—with universal values, with a message of peace among men, and with distinctive principles of social and political organization—exerts an influence upon the policy-making decisions of its followers, its influence is felt primarily in those areas to which its teachings have immediate relevance. When a Muslim statesman confronts a gigantic struggle such as the Cold War—in which questions of sociopolitical organizations are said to occupy a prominent position, and in which grave dangers to the peace and indeed the very survival of the world lurk—it is natural, therefore, to expect that the distinctive influence of Islam should express itself in the first instance in a typically Islamic "ideological" or "doctrinaire" approach to the struggle.

Yet, what is happening is the exact opposite of what we might expect. Far from distinguishing themselves for their original contributions to ideological or doctrinaire neutralism, Muslim neutralists have on the whole represented the simplest form of nationalist-pragmatic neutralism.

Leadership in establishing the *doctrinaire* grounds of neutralist policy has come from outside the ranks of Muslim statesmanship, particularly from Hindu and Buddhist statesmen. The attempts made by some Indian scholars to link their country's neutralism to its spiritual and intellectual heritage succeed, in my layman's opinion, in tracing the origins of some Nehruvian policies to deep-rooted religious and cultural Indian traditions. When a few Muslim leaders—notably Sukarno, Nāṣir, and Sékou Touré—began somewhat belatedly to inject some doctrinaire elements into their neutralist views, they did so, as the terminology and conceptual content of their expositions clearly demonstrate, not by drawing inspiration from the spiritual heritage of Islam but by echoing the words and paraphrasing the thoughts of non-Muslim neutralists, especially Nehru. The majority of Muslim neutralist leaders, however, have remained impervious to the doctrinaire factor in neutralism.

The *ideological* element also was lacking in the neutralism of Muslim regimes during the initial and formative periods. When hints of an ideological rationale began to appear, they were not only late blooms but perhaps also afterthoughts. It was not because they had already erected independent ideological constructions of their own that they chose to be politically neutral in the Cold War; it was after, and possibly because, they had already chosen political neutrality in the East-West conflict (for nationalist-pragmatic reasons) that some Muslim neutralists sought to develop independent indigenous socioeconomic systems.

More significantly, the ideological formulations of Muslim neutralists evince striking similarity to the systems or themes propounded by their non-Muslim fellow-neutralists and lack the hallmarks of Islamic lineage.

It is not Islam, nor some Islamic system, that Muslim neutralists, when ideologically motivated, submit as the alternative to the contending philosophies or systems of East and West. It is not in the name of Islam as a religion that they utter their "neither-nor." Nor is it in accordance with some Islamic recipe that they propose to formulate their independent sociopolitical system. The alternative they offer to the battling ideologies of the Cold War is *socialism.* But, be it remembered, it is "*Arab* socialism," "*Indonesian* socialism," or "*African* socialism" that they proclaim—not "*Islamic* socialism."

The Cold War has a dual ideological aspect: it is a debate between two outlooks on life, history, and human destiny, and a competition between two social systems. Muslim leaders, who as Muslims are heirs to a distinctive Islamic outlook on life and reality, fail to propose Islam as their theological, metaphysical, or moral alternative to the *Weltanschauung* of East or West and therefore as the basis of their ideological neutralism. At the same time, they fail to cultivate the rudiments of social philosophy implicit in Islamic doctrines, to adapt them to the conditions of modern life, and to adopt the resultant construction as their chosen system of social reorganization and as a mark of their independent orientation in world affairs. In short, they confront the Cold War as ideological neutralists, with an "ideology" that lacks Islamic spiritual foundation and philosophical backbone, whose socio-economic content is non-Islamic, and whose character they authoritatively identify in *nationalist,* not religious, terms.

Socialism, of one kind or another, has spread rapidly in neutralist countries in the past few years. Today, eight Muslim neutralist regimes profess themselves to be socialistic; and socialism is established or advancing in six non-Muslim neutralist countries. (See Table II.) The leaders of these countries are also the most articulately ideological of neutralists. Socialism has thus become the basis of ideological neutralism. The relation of Islam to socialism is therefore an important index of the relevance of Islam to neutralism.

Independent and comparative studies of the rise and nature of socialism in the self-styled "socialist" countries of Asia, Africa, and the Arab world are urgently called for. On the basis of preliminary studies, however, the following observations can be made:

1. According to the leaders directly concerned, the factors that have prevailed in, and have occasioned the transition to socialism of, the socialist-neutralist countries of Asia, Africa, and the Arab world have been similar in nature to one another and common to all those countries, Muslim and non-Muslim alike.

2. These factors have been related primarily to the social and economic conditions, the internal and international

political situation, and the psychological mood (rising popular aspirations) of those countries, rather than to preconceived ideas or dogmas. Afro-Asian–Arab socialism has been more or less pragmatic, not dogmatic, in its rise and evolution.

3. Where dogmas have entered the picture at all, they have been non-Islamic dogmas (e.g., Marxism).

4. The lines along which these forms of socialism have evolved have been virtually parallel, notwithstanding the Muslim character of the leadership and population of some of the countries in question and the non-Muslim nature of others. Where there has been divergence, it has been caused by peculiar national circumstances, not by religious dissimilarity.

5. Many of the popular or intellectual movements that have paved the way for the adoption of socialism in Muslim countries have been either openly or implicitly secular in nature and leadership. Some have been inspired or led by non-Muslims.

6. Muslim socialist leaders have made some efforts, which have borne close resemblance to efforts made by non-Muslim socialists in the Afro-Asian–Arab community, to show the *national* character of their brands of socialism, and to emphasize the organic relationship between the new institutions they have been fashioning and their respective national traditions.

7. Muslim socialist leaders have made other efforts, also resembling the efforts of non-Muslim socialists in the area, to justify the establishment of socialism in terms of practical, local values and "scientific" principles. The wisdom, the desirability, and, according to some, the "inevitability" of the "socialist solution" have been defended on the basis of: (a) practical assessment of the national resources and of the realistic prospects of development; (b) a presumed general desire for enhancing the well-being and serving the interest

of the nation and its component individuals and groups; (c) "scientific principles" of social organization; and (d) universally recognized humanistic values (e.g., "social justice") which, while not incompatible with Islam, are far from being exclusively Muslim.

8. No serious effort has been made by Muslim socialist leaders (except perhaps in Algeria) to trace the origin of their chosen forms of socialism to Islamic doctrines or traditions, or to ascribe their distinguishing features to Islamic inspiration.

9. That some Muslim leaders have sought to reconcile socialism with Islam cannot be gainsaid. But it will be observed that generally the purpose has been to demonstrate the lack of incompatibility between Islamic and socialist aims, not the derivation of socialism from Islam. The dominant mood in such "apologetics" of socialism has been somewhat defensive; and the efforts to prove the consonance of Islam and socialism have generally been preceded, and perhaps stimulated, by charges of dissonance and incompatibility.

In short, as far as their choice of roads to neutralism is concerned, Muslim neutralists have shown a general tendency, manifested also by non-Muslims, to favor the *nationalist-pragmatic* highway. Those who have taken the *doctrinaire* path have been relatively few; and in any case they have done so at a late stage in the journey, after they had already arrived at the neutralist assembly hall. Their experience has been in the nature of a side excursion, probably prompted by the example, if not by the inducement, of non-Muslim pioneers. Another excursion, which has proved somewhat more attractive to Muslim neutralists, has taken them along the *ideological* trail. However, those Muslim leaders who have taken this side trip have returned to the neutralist assembly hall with glowing reports about the non-Islamic landmarks they saw, as though the sight of Islamic landmarks had entirely escaped them.

We encounter a similar situation when we turn to the second group of categories, namely, the varieties of neutralist orientation. For here too what we expect to find and what we do find, by way of Islamic influence, are vastly different.

The dedication to justice, law, order, and peace, which Islam infuses into the faithful, might be expected to predispose Muslim statesmen to an active diplomacy of peacemaking, such as characterizes messianic neutralism. Alternatively, the fact that Islam furnishes the believer with a *Weltanschauung* and a *Weltansicht* of its own might lead one to expect that, confronted with a Cold War between two ways of life, both alien to Islam, Muslims would express their neutrality vis-à-vis that competition in disinterest and indifference, that is, in passive neutralism. And yet, contrary to both expectations, it is neither *messianic* nor *passive* neutralism that has characterized the orientation of most Muslim neutralists. The most common forms of expression of neutralism in Muslim countries have been *negative* neutralism, or nonalignment, and *positive* neutralism.

Passive neutralism has been as unenduring among Muslim neutralists as among their non-Muslim counterparts, and as negligible.

And the *messianic* exercises in earnest peacemaking, to which a few Muslim neutralists have applied themselves in recent years, have been conducted largely in company with non-Muslim neutralists, who had begun to apply themselves to the task years earlier. The techniques and methods employed have been the same as those originally introduced by the non-Muslim trail blazers. And the system of world order that those exercises have aimed at establishing can hardly be traced, in its conceptual and axiological lineage, to the classical theory of international relations formulated during the creative period of Islamic history, when Islamic thought and policy relating to international affairs came into their own.

The vision of world order with which messianic neutralists

confront the philosophy of the Cold War (and in accordance with which they shape their diplomatic initiatives, aimed at the resolution of specific problems stemming from the Cold War) is a vision of a bloc-free, pluralistic world of free nations: all equal in sovereign rights and in dignity, despite inequality in size, fortunes, power, and technological attainments; all coexisting in a framework of free intercourse, in spite of vast differences among their cherished social systems and outlooks on life; and all collaborating with one another within a universal organization, submitting to universal norms governing international conduct, and accepting the principle of pacific settlement of international disputes. This vision is a far cry indeed from the Islamic vision of the world that animated thought and statesmanship in the era of Islamic vitality and Muslim power. In fact, it is the Cold War philosophy, and not the philosophy of messianic neutralism, that bears resemblance to the classical Islamic theory of international relations.

IV

The three lines of investigation have, individually and independently of one another, pointed to—and have, I believe, jointly established—one conclusion: that *Islam is irrelevant to neutralism.*

This irrelevance is manifested in several ways, which have been indicated already, but which may now be summed up in the following propositions:

1. Neutralism is the chosen foreign policy of several Muslim governments; but it is neither common to all Muslim states nor restricted to them. Not all Muslims are neutralist, nor are all neutralists Muslim.

2. Greater similarity obtains between the patterns of thought and action, regarding international affairs, of Muslim and non-Muslim neutralists (and of Muslim and non-

Muslim counterneutralists) than between the international thinking and conduct of the two groups of Muslims.

3. (a) When Muslims exercise neutralism, they do so in ways that are neither (i) uniform nor (ii) essentially and typically Islamic nor (iii) peculiar to, and distinctive of, Islamic statesmanship.

(b) When some Muslims favor certain forms of neutralism over others, they usually show preference for those forms in which the influence of Islam is least likely to be felt—namely, nationalist-pragmatic motivation, and negative or negative-positive orientation.

(c) Even when some Muslims choose those forms of neutralism upon which Islam may be expected to exercise a significant influence (namely, doctrinaire or ideological motivation, and passive or messianic orientation), they usually give expression, in their utterances and deeds, to ideas, principles, and values that are either (i) extraneous to Islam or (ii) universal, and therefore shared by non-Islamic and Islamic traditions.

4. When Muslim leaders plead for (or when they expostulate against) neutralism, they usually do so in non-Islamic terms.

5. The causes that most commonly occasion the adoption of neutralism (or counterneutralism) by Muslim statesmen are nationalistic, not religious, in nature. So are the objectives most commonly sought through the chosen policy. Those causes and objectives are equally decisive in the policy-making experience of non-Muslim statesmen as well.

6. The espousal (or rejection) of neutralism by Muslim leaders and their profession of Islam appear, therefore, to have nothing to do with each other. Muslim leaders seem to decide for (or against) neutralism as if they believed that Islam gave its followers no guidance in the domain of foreign-policy making. Their behavior appears to indicate that, in their opinion, Islam neither prohibits nor commends neutralism.

7. One may conclude, then, that (a) Islam, as interpreted and practiced by Muslim statesmen, is "neutral" in the debate between neutralism and counterneutralism, and that (b) neutralism is neither essentially Islamic nor incompatible with Islam, but indifferent to that faith.

V

We have focused our attention so far on Islam as it appears to be interpreted and practiced by contemporary Muslims. This may give rise to some questions:

Is Islam, as it is understood and observed by the present generation of Muslims, an authentic version of its original self? And is it the only possible version?

Are the thoughts and actions of contemporary Muslims the best source, or the sole source, of Islamic theory—whether in relation to international affairs or to other fields? Are not the literature and practice of the classical period of Islamic history a more fitting (and perhaps a more fecund) source?

Is not the assertion of the irrelevance of Islam to neutralism, and the implied irrelevance of Islam to foreign policy in general, in the context of present international reality—predicated as that assertion is on the equation of "contemporary Islam" with "Islam as such"—strictly confined in its validity to the former?

Let me say in all candor that, in the context of a symposium on "Islam and International Relations" such as this, the only acceptation of the term "Islam" which I consider meaningful is that which the community of living Muslims understands and observes. Only the faith that is accepted and lived by its followers can be a factor in their conduct, and worthy of study as such. To the extent to which Islamic theories and traditions, developed in a past era, do not appear to today's Muslims to be relevant factors in their own international life and in their day-to-day decisions on foreign affairs, to that extent those theories and traditions cease to have practical significance for the analysis of policy- and decision-making in the world of the present. (It goes without saying, however, that the academic or historical value of those theories or traditions, and their intrinsic spiritual worth, remain unaffected by their loss of practical, current relevance.)

Moreover, my concern in this subject is descriptive, not normative. The question I ask myself is, "How *does* Islam actually affect (or, perhaps, how *may* it affect) the conduct of Muslims?"—not, "How *should* Islam influence the behavior of the believers?"

Apart from all this, however, I submit that an examination of the contemporary relevance to international relations of the classical Islamic theories, even as modified and adjusted in postclassical times, would yield the same negative results which our three-pronged investigation of contemporary Islam has indicated.

For the international setting within which those theories developed has been demolished by history and replaced by a fundamentally dissimilar setting. The destruction of the realities and patterns of power, and the elimination of those forms of action that they had made possible or expedient have in turn destroyed the foundation of the classical Islamic theories of international relations and left them in a state of total inapplicability to modern world conditions.

In order to revive those theories, to bring them up to date, to adapt them to present-day conditions, and to endow them with some measure of current applicability, Islamic political theorists cannot proceed by endeavoring to reconstruct a demolished edifice or to build new layers on top of razed foundations. They must rather sweep aside what tempests have ruined and time has eroded, and start afresh—drawing inspiration from the same spiritual fountain whence their predecessors had derived the principles they applied to the circumstances under which they lived, but applying those principles to their own circumstances creatively, unfettered by traditional forms or precepts.

Until Islamic jurists and political theorists embark upon such a process of re-creation, or unless the present realities of power and the structures of public life in the world are magically transformed so as to resemble the patterns of international actuality that obtained when the classical Islamic theories of international relations came into their own, a yawning chasm will continue to separate the theories of yesterday from the realities and tasks of today. And the classical Islamic theories of international relations will remain irrelevant and inapplicable to the actual conduct of Muslim statesmen.

In the internal organization of society, a Muslim leader may or may not follow a secular approach. If he chooses to remain faithful to the traditional socio-economic concepts of Islam, and to draw inspiration from them in his decisions and actions, he may be able to derive some meaningful guidance from Islamic teachings and values and from past Islamic experiences. If, on the other hand, he chooses to follow a secular approach, and to decide upon his courses of action in terms of what he considers possible, expedient, useful, and (according to his best lights) morally right, he may succeed in shaping policies and formulating programs that are not necessarily incompatible with the spirit of Islam nor irreconcilable with the example of past generations of Muslims. Secularism and nonsecularism are therefore two options that are equally available to him, and the respective consequences of which are not necessarily irreconcilable.

In international affairs, however, only one option is possible. A Muslim statesman has no choice but to be secular; that is to say, he must plan and make decisions without validating his choices in terms of an authoritative body of doctrines and a set of model experiences associated with a sacred past and a sacrosanct tradition.

However profoundly committed he may be to the proposition that Islam governs both man and society—that is, however nonsecular his approach to internal national affairs—a Muslim statesman is bound to act in international affairs as though he were secularly oriented. He is compelled to ignore traditional Islamic theories of international affairs. The only alternative to secularism in international relations that is available to a Muslim today is for him to "live and move and have his being" in an unreal world, and to think in terms of obsolete theories which do not, and cannot, have the slightest bearing on the reality that envelops him.

NOTES

1. Lebanon is the only member of the League of Arab States that is not a "Muslim country."

2. The text of the official communiqué may be found in *The Conference of Heads of State or Government of Non-Aligned Countries* (Accra, Ghana: Ministry of Information, 1961), pp. 15–16. The passage quoted appears in par. 3, p. 15.

3. "Non-Aligned Preparatory Conference Meets in Cairo," *Arab Review* (Cairo), Vol. 2 (June, 1961), pp. 11–13.

4. *Ibid.*

5. In addition to the twenty-five countries listed in the text, three countries (Bolivia, Brazil, and Ecuador) were represented by observers.

6. Elsewhere, the present author discusses more fully the typology of neutralism sketched in the following paragraphs. See "Anatomy of Neutralism," *The Dynamics of Neutralism in the Arab World*, ed. F. A. Sayegh (San Francisco, 1964).

The Significance of Religion in Arab Nationalism

By Bayard Dodge

"Before Muḥammad there were the Arabs and before Christ there were the Arabs." This was a slogan adopted by Amir Faysal for Arabs of all religious sects when he led his victorious troops into Syria at the end of World War I.

In spite of this political appeal, Arab nationalism has increasingly become identified with Islam. The great majority of the Jews who once lived in Iraq, the Yemen, Egypt, and North Africa have migrated to Israel. The Greek and Syrian Orthodox Christians, as well as the Copts and Armenians, have adopted a policy of cooperation with their Muslim neighbors, while the foreigners in North Africa and Egypt have to a great extent returned to Europe. Although Lebanon is unique, with a Maronite president of the republic and a population that is half Christian, the country is too small to exert a decisive influence among the Muslims in the Middle East as a whole.

When, therefore, religion is mentioned in connection with Arab nationalism, it is inevitably the faith of Islam. In order to appreciate the significance of this statement, it is necessary to recall why Islam became connected with affairs of a national and political character.

I. The Theocracy of Islam

To begin with, Islam had no connection with nationalism, but was a spiritual and moral movement to cleanse the land from idolatry and polytheism. After Muḥammad had seen a vision and heard a voice calling him to become a prophet, he lived for a number of years at Mecca, where he challenged the pagan Arabs to abandon their idols and to escape the fire of hell by righteous living.[1]

Many of the early passages of the Qur'ān contain the following warning:

> Lo! the Day of Decision is a fixed time, a day when the trumpet is blown and ye come in multitudes, and the heaven is opened and becometh as gates. . . . Lo! hell lurketh in ambush, a home for the rebellious. They will abide therein for ages.[2]
>
> Lo! Ours is to give guidance. . . . Therefore I have warned you of the flaming Fire. . . . Far removed from it will be the righteous who giveth of his wealth, purifying himself.[3]

Examples of this sort make it evident that Islam did not begin as a national or political movement, but rather as a spiritual revival and an appeal for social reform. During the year 622, however, a well-known event led to new developments among the Muslim converts. The people of the agricultural center, destined to be known as al-Madīnah, came to the conclusion that they should bring to an end the discord wrecking the life of their community. In this small center there were eleven principal clans, three of which were Jewish and eight Arab. The large Arab groups of Aws and Khazraj were fomenting political jealousy, while the small clans were so individualistic in spirit that there was constant friction. In order to achieve a greater degree of cooperation, representatives of these groups invited the Prophet Muḥammad to end their rivalries by exerting his spiritual leadership. When the Prophet went on his famous *Hijrah* to al-Madīnah, Islam became something more than a spiritual and social revival; it became a theocracy.

At al-Madīnah Muḥammad took the place of a parliament as he legislated laws by Qur'ānic revelation. He served as the judiciary, for important cases were brought to him for legal decision. He was also the executive power, since the people delegated to him both the administration of their tribal affairs and relationships with foreign rulers.

The Prophet, however, was more interested in spreading spiritual and social reform than in political imperialism. ". . . Allah will perfect His light however much the disbelievers are averse. He it is who hath sent His messenger with the guidance and the religion of truth, that He may make it the conqueror of all religion." [4]

When, moreover, a man asked Muḥammad, "What is patriotism?" the Prophet replied, "That thou assist thy people in spite of their wrongdoing." [5]

Even when the Muslim realm was expanded by Muḥammad's successors from the Pamirs to the Pyrenees, it was more like a confederation of peoples, held together by a common faith and culture, than a modern nation-state. With tribal chiefs and autonomous governors in far-flung provinces, the

Muslim empire of the Middle Ages was held together not so much by centralized control as by loyalty to the Caliph, who was regarded as having the divine right to defend Islam and to enforce the laws revealed by God. Thus medieval Islam encouraged international brotherhood rather than provincial nationalism.

In spite of this international spirit, however, there must have been emotions similar to those of modern nationalism when Arab soldiers went forth to defend Islam against the Byzantine armies. When, moreover, the capital was at Baghdad, Arab superiority was so threatened by a flood of foreign merchants, scholars, slaves, and soldiers of fortune pouring into Mesopotamia from distant lands that a spirit of race consciousness developed among the families of Arab descent.

At the same time Islam itself was menaced, since many of the foreign proselytes did not entirely abandon the memories learned in childhood before conversion. Muslim traditions were constantly in danger of becoming confused with those of the Christians, Jews, Zoroastrians, and Manichaeans. Fearing, therefore, a loss of both social prestige and religious orthodoxy, the Arabs became bound together by a communal spirit, inspired by loyalty to their race and to the true revelations of the Qur'ān.

Although this racial consciousness differed from the nationalism of later times, it was destined to become more pronounced because of the series of misfortunes that befell the Arabs during the Middle Ages.

II. Foreign Oppression

During the year 945, when the foreign chieftain Aḥmad ibn-Buwayh occupied Baghdad, the tottering Arab caliphate suffered a serious collapse. Losing all temporal power, the Caliph became a puppet in the hands of his military conquerors, serving merely as a symbol of Islamic theocracy. Instead of being members of a ruling class, the Arabs became the subjects of foreign adventurers. Their position was not improved when, at the same time that William the Conqueror was invading England, the Saljūq Turks occupied Iraq. Humiliation came not only from the Asiatic tribes but also from the West. After occupying Jerusalem in 1099, the Crusaders filled two centuries with threats against the independence of the Arab population as well as against Islam itself.

During the Crusades there was one aspect of Muslim Arab psychology which is just as significant at the present time as it was centuries ago. This matter is well explained by an event that occurred in medieval Egypt:

During the thirteenth century King Louis IX of France, better known as St. Louis, led a crusade against the Nile Valley, hoping to prevent the Sultan in Cairo from sending supplies and reinforcements to the Saracen armies in Palestine. After seizing the port of Damietta, the Crusaders fought their way up the Nile as far as al-Mansurah.

At this time the last important member of the dynasty founded by Saladin (Ṣalāḥ al-Dīn Yūsuf ibn-Ayyūb) was ruling Egypt. Although he was a Muslim, he was descended from Kurdish rather than Arab forebears. His famous queen, Shajar al-Durr, was by origin a foreign concubine, while his palace guard was composed of slaves from Central Asia. Being subject to these foreign masters, one would have supposed that the Egyptians would have welcomed a new regime with hopes of a greater degree of social equality. What actually happened, however, was that the members of the exploited Egyptian population far preferred to be ruled by a Muslim despot than by a Christian saint.

In one of his well-known books, a medieval historian recorded that on "Friday a proclamation was brought to Cairo from the military camp, inciting the people to a holy war." It began with a famous verse from the Qur'ān, "March forth, light or heavy, and persevere in the path of Allah both with your possessions and yourselves, for this is what is best for you." According to the historian, "When it was read to the people from the pulpit of the Mosque of Cairo, its recital brought forth tears, lamentation, and a raising of voices in a tumult, which cannot be described." [6]

It was not long afterward that St. Louis was taken prisoner and his troops were obliged to evacuate Egypt. When Queen Shajar al-Durr celebrated this victory in Cairo, the rejoicing of the people was both exuberant and sincere, for the most important aspect of their nationalism was a desire to defend the integrity of their faith.

From the time of St. Louis until the beginning of the sixteenth century, the Arabs of the Middle East were for the most part ruled by foreign sultans known as Mamlūks. A Mamlūk was a slave boy purchased from the tribes of Central Asia or the Caucasus, trained to be a cavalryman, and frequently assigned to military and administrative work. Although these officers were slaves by origin, they had complete control over the Arab population. In each generation the most important Mamlūk became a sultan, with power to rule as a military tyrant, supported by his Mamlūk cavalry. These foreign officers spoke their own dialects and treated the Arabic-speaking peasants as second-class citizens, whom they exploited in a brutal way. When the Ottoman Turks gained control over the Arab provinces at the beginning of the sixteenth century, Turkish was naturally the language of the ruling class. Many of the Mamlūks were still employed for government work and the Arabs continued to be humiliated.

For certain types of work, however, the Arabs were indispensable. Since it was unanimously accepted by all Muslims that Allah revealed the Qur'ān in Arabic, there was no desire to translate it into any other language. Because, moreover, Muslim law, theology, worship, and education depended upon the Qur'ān, only Arabs well versed in their own culture were capable of serving as judges, lawyers, notaries, mosque leaders, prayer callers, Qur'ānic reciters, professors, and schoolteachers. Thus, although the Arabs were subject to foreign masters, they did have important roles to play in their own communities.

Needless to say, the legal authorities were influential, for marriage and divorce, inheritance, the establishing of pious foundations, the punishing of crimes, and business transactions of all sorts depended upon the law. Mosque leaders were also in demand, since thousands of worshipers crowded into the mosques for Friday prayers and, especially during Ramaḍān, large groups gathered together to hear the Qur'ān recited and explained. Public gatherings, moreover, as well as circumcisions, weddings, and funerals, were accompanied by religious rites. Great numbers of Arabs, therefore, gained an honorable livelihood and social prestige by working in the law courts and mosques.

It became necessary to develop a vast system of education, which was encouraged by the rulers, since they needed well-trained men for their judicial work. Although the education was completely medieval in character, centered in the mosques and religious colleges, it was so thorough that it produced many first-class scholars.

The Turks also encouraged the ascetics and mystics, who maintained a policy of political acquiescence, leaving worldly affairs to their governors while they themselves sought reward in the life hereafter. Many of the foreign officials bestowed generous endowments on the dervisheries, while they encouraged Sūfi scholars to teach in the mosques and colleges.

Because the religious and legal authorities were the only influential members of the Arab population, they became the recognized leaders of the poorer classes, obliged to serve as mediators between the exploited populace and the foreign rulers. Thus whatever Arab nationalism existed was closely bound to religious influences. The important point to bear in mind is that during centuries of Ottoman rule Islam depended upon the Arabs, while at the same time the prestige and self-preservation of the Arabs depended upon Islam.

At the end of the eighteenth century the Ottomans permitted two Mamlūk officers to govern Egypt, granting them an undue amount of local autonomy. So much brutality and corruption existed that the Arabic-speaking population was in the depths of despair. When Napoleon Bonaparte invaded Egypt, he used psychological warfare, proclaiming that he was coming to release the population from the tyranny of these Mamlūk governors. At the same time he was astute enough to make it known that he wished to uphold Islam, rather than to undermine its influence.

Napoleon's private secretary has quoted the following proclamation, which the general issued to the people of Egypt when in 1798 he landed his expeditionary force on the beach near Alexandria:

> People of Egypt—you will be told that I am come to destroy your religion—do not believe it. Be assured that I am come to restore your rights, to punish the usurpers, and that I respect, more than the Mamluks, God, his prophet and the Alcoran. Tell them that all men are equal in the eye of God: wisdom, talents and virtue make the only difference. Cadis, sheikhs, imams, scorbajis, tell the people that we are friends of the true Mussulmans. Have not we destroyed the pope, who says that war ought to be made upon Mussulmans? Have we not destroyed the knights of Malta, because those bigots believed that God required them to raise their swords against the Mussulmans? [7]

After forcing his way up the Nile and entering Cairo, Bonaparte notified the public:

> There shall be in each province of Egypt a divan, composed of seven individuals; whose duty shall be to superintend the interests of the province; to communicate to me any complaints that may be made; to prevent warfare among the different vil-

lages; to apprehend and punish criminals . . . ; and to take every opportunity of enlightening the people.[8]

In Cairo the Great Divan was established as an advisory council, composed of ten Muslim legal and religious authorities with the rector of the university mosque of al-Azhar as the presiding officer. The formation of these councils was an effort to give the Egyptians themselves a share in the administration of the land and also an attempt to honor Islam as their official faith.

In spite of these efforts to win the confidence of the population, Napoleon's expedition was so unsuccessful that in October, 1801, there were no more French troops left in Egypt. Religion and nationalism were so closely bound together that the people refused to submit to the rule of a non-Muslim suzerain, even though he was the greatest genius of his age, claiming to be a champion of social justice and Islam. The attachment between nationalism and religion was just as strong at the time of Bonaparte as it had been during the days of St. Louis.

The shock of Napoleon's invasion was followed by a number of events that awakened the Arabs from the stagnation of Ottoman times. This early renaissance was largely due to the ambitious measures of Muḥammad 'Alī and the Khedive Ismā'īl. It was also encouraged by the influence of foreign schools and the obtaining of Arab autonomy in the forward-looking province of Mount Lebanon.

One of the leaders of this awakening did not come from Europe or the Near East, but from far-off Afghanistan. In 1871 Jamāl al-Dīn al-Afghānī arrived in Cairo. He was an Afghan who had studied in Persia and India before he moved to Egypt. His tremendous vitality and progressive ideas attracted scores of students to his home, where he taught precepts of a revolutionary character. Although he did not preach a doctrine of Arab nationalism, he strongly emphasized the necessity to free the Muslims from foreign rule in countries like India, the Sudan, and those of North Africa. At the same time he called upon the youth to revive their religion in the light of modern scientific thought, so as once again to make Islam a world power. After living in Egypt for eight years, he went to Paris where he issued his famous revolutionary journal, *al-'Urwah al-Wuthqā.*

Two of his admirers carried on his work in an especially conspicuous way. One of them was Shaykh Muḥammad 'Abduh, who was largely responsible for the intellectual awakening in Egypt; the other was the national leader, Sa'd Zaghlul. The first of these men was a religious reformer conscious of the importance of nationalism, while the other was a political rebel whose religious training made it impossible for him to forget Islam.

While Egypt was emerging from the lethargy of Ottoman times, the Sudan became the center of a movement that demonstrated in a striking way how closely nationalism is bound to religion. In 1881 the Mahdī inaugurated his great revolution. The wretched Sudanese were ready for revolt. Although their foreign rulers had employed a few honest administrators like Baker and Gordon, most of their governors had been Turkish-speaking officers bent on enriching themselves by exploitation and slave-dealing. When the revolution occurred, it was not only a nationalistic demand for freedom but also an outburst of religious emotion. The Mahdī did not promise his followers material welfare in the present world, but demanded sacrifice, assuring his zealous tribesmen of rich rewards in the world to come.

Illustrations of this sort make it evident that the embryonic nationalism, which developed before the end of the nineteenth century, was invariably linked with religion. At the same time that the Arabs were appealing for social justice and political freedom, they were also striving to uphold the supremacy of their religious faith.

III. Islam and Independence

During World War I, when the Ottomans declared a holy war against the Allies, instead of rallying to the call of the Sultan, the Arabs revolted against the Turks, demanding the right to enjoy their own Arab nationalism and independence. Although the Arab revolt was opposed to the holy war, it was nevertheless related to Islam, since the leader of the Arabs was Grand Sharīf Ḥusayn of Mecca, a descendant of the Prophet Muḥammad and guardian of the holy Muslim shrines.

Promises made by the British during the war, followed by Woodrow Wilson's Fourteen Points advocating self-determination, crystallized Arab nationalism into a definite movement. Two examples make it clear that this ferment was not divorced from religion.

In the first place, the son of Grand Sharīf Ḥusayn was accepted first as the ruler of Syria and later as King Fayṣal I of Iraq. Although he was an orthodox Sunnī who belonged to a tribal family of Arabia and was neither Syrian nor Iraqi, even the heterodox Ismā'īlīyah of Syria and Shī'ah of Iraq acclaimed him, because he was a lineal descendant of Muḥammad. Local attachments were less important than loyalty to the family of the Prophet.

In the second place, when there was a widespread revolution against the British in Egypt during the years 1919 and 1920, the religious shaykhs played an important part in the revolt, the Mosque of al-Azhar serving as one of the principle centers of the rebellion.

Even more significant than these examples is the mention of Islam in the constitutions of the Arab states. Titre VI, Art. 149, of the Egyptian constitution of 1923 reads, "L'Islam est la religion de l'Etat; l'Arabe est sa langue officielle."

Part I, Art. 3, of the constitution of 1956 contains the same statement.

The constitution of Iraq, first promulgated in 1924 and revised in 1943, states in Part I, Art. 13, "Islam is the official religion of the state." In the same way the constitution adopted by King 'Abdallāh in 1946–47 specifies in Art. 2 of the introduction, "The Hashemite Kingdom of Transjordan is an independent, sovereign and free state. Its religion is Islam."

The constitution adopted by Syria in 1950 also stipulated in Chap. I, Art. 3, "The religion of the President of the Republic is Islam. Islamic law shall be the main source of legislation."

In order to avoid misunderstanding, it should be explained that when Islam is adopted as the religion of the state it does not imply disregard for religious liberty. Thus the preliminary constitution adopted by the leaders of the Egyptian revolution in 1956 states in Part III, Art. 43, "Freedom of worship is unrestricted. The State guarantees free religious observance, in accordance with the established usage in Egypt, provided this does not conflict with public order or morality." Similar clauses appear in the other constitutions.

During the period of renaissance following World War I, both Arab nationalism and the religion of Islam were subjected to bitter humiliation. All of the Arab lands were either occupied by foreign armies or exposed to the economic and diplomatic interference of the Western Powers. Although Egypt was declared to be independent, a British garrison remained in the country, the Suez Canal continued to be conducted as a foreign enterprise, and the business of the kingdom was largely controlled by foreign corporations. In other lands, most of the public utilities and transport companies, as well as the huge petroleum industries, were also exploited by foreign financiers.

In 1924 Atatürk discontinued the historic caliphate, leaving the Muslims without even a symbol of their theocracy. Because of the Treaty of Sèvres and subsequent negotiations, the assurances given to the Arabs in the correspondence between Sir Henry McMahon and Grand Sharīf Ḥusayn in 1915 and 1916 seemed to be disregarded. Palestine, Jordan, Lebanon, Syria, and Iraq were placed under mandates, while the Zionists were offered an entering wedge in regions that had been occupied by Arab farmers for many centuries.

The mandated territories met with varied fortunes, but in general the Arabs felt that they were obliged to suffer from economic exploitation and political interference. Except for a few foreign enterprises, industry was discouraged so as to prevent competition with European factories. Such large shares of the state revenues were required to pay the salaries of foreign officials that it was impossible to do justice to agriculture, education, and public health. Not only in Algeria, but also in numerous other states, the Muslims felt that they were discriminated against in an unfair way, favor being shown to members of the minority sects.

When the United Nations organization was formed, the people of the Middle East hoped that at last their aspirations might be realized. They were encouraged by Chap. I, Art. 1, par. 3, of the Charter, which states that one of the purposes of the United Nations is "To develop friendly relations among nations based on respect for the principles of equal rights and self-determination of peoples, and to take other appropriate measures to strengthen universal peace."

One of the steps first taken by the United Nations turned this spirit of confidence into cynicism, changing hope into despair and patience into anger. When the state of Israel was formed, members of the Arab youth were seized by a passionate desire to regain the honor of Arab nationalism and the prestige of Islam. The opposition to foreigners in Egypt, Syria, and Iraq; the aid given to rebels in Algeria; the nationalization of the Suez Canal; and the increase of propaganda in foreign lands reveal the spirit of this resentment.

In 1928 Shaykh Ḥasan al-Bannā' founded an organization called the Muslim Brothers, or *Ikhwān al-Muslimūn,* with the purpose of purifying and vitalizing Islam. When he was killed during the year that followed the partition of Palestine, his successor allowed the members to become interested in political nationalism as well as in religion. Thousands of young men, incited by the humiliations inflicted upon the Arabs and Islam, joined in the movement, thus fusing their nationalism and religious faith. It was only when the Egyptian revolution occurred in 1952 that the enthusiasm of the youth was channeled into other forms of activity. The Muslim Brothers hoped to revive their national life and religion by going back to the institutions of early Islam; the founders of the Egyptian revolution do not look backward, but forward.

IV. Modernism

At the same time that they are obtaining independence, the Arab Muslims are passing through an intellectual revolution. Muslim law, for instance, was suited to the needs of the Middle Ages, but is no longer applicable to most of the usages of modern life. Banking and insurance, industry and transportation, advertising, and other fields of work are not provided for. Even family life is changing so much that the ancient laws for marriage, divorce, and inheritance require new interpretations. The old punishments, moreover, are out of date, as it does not seem to be humane to cut off the hand of a thief or to prescribe a hundred lashes for adultery. Accordingly, the great legal system based upon the Qur'ān and the traditions of the Prophet is being supplemented by modern law codes.

At the same time, the ancient rites and practices do not seem to be in keeping with the modern world. It is true that the uneducated men still observe the five daily prayers and crowd into the mosques every Friday. They keep the fast of Ramaḍān and do their best to go to Mecca at least once in a lifetime. On the whole they are careful to refrain from drinking liquor, eating pig's meat, and gambling, doing their best to observe the Qur'ānic ordinances. On the other hand, the educated members of the younger generation no longer regard these rules and ceremonies as important. They dislike the bodily movements used in prayer, they see no harm in eating ham and drinking beer, and they delight in betting at the horse races and ball games.

Almost all of the Arab countries have developed extensive systems of secular education to take the place of the old mosque classes. Not only elementary schools but also *lycées* and universities are being established in many of the more important cities. In Cairo alone there are 75,000 students in well-equipped and highly organized university departments. What is especially significant is that many of these new institutions are coeducational.

As the newly liberated states need armies for defense and industries for economic development, there is a great emphasis upon science and technology. Accordingly, the educated boys and girls no longer depend upon the Qur'ān to supply solutions to life's problems. More and more they are neglecting the orthodox sources of religion, substituting modern textbooks for ancient scriptures.

A number of leaders have tried to help the youth to understand religion in a constructive way. Sir Muḥammad Iqbāl courageously interpreted historical dogmas in accord with modern science. He suggested that passages in the Qur'ān about predestination, Adam and Eve, heaven and hell should be understood in a spiritual rather than a literal way. He said that prayer, "whether individual or associative, is an expression of man's inner yearning for a response in the awful silence of the universe." He also stated that the action of a legislative assembly, rather than the consensus of the scholars, might interpret Islamic law so as to adapt it to modern needs.[9] Iqbāl was interested in reviving Islam, instead of in provincial nationalism. What he desired was to formulate a philosophy that would erase the narrow loyalties of nationalism, awaken the people of Islam "from the torpor of a despondent fatalism and stir them to activity in the name of the heritage of dynamic ideals." [10]

In spite of the efforts of Iqbāl and other progressive thinkers, the educated young Arabs tend to neglect the intellectual aspects of Islam and to express their emotions in terms of a narrow nationalism, rather than of religion. As a student from Arabia said in one of my seminars, "My religion is nationalism."

For many centuries the caliphs tried to expand the Islamic territories by means of the holy war. Today all seem to agree that the *jihād* should be used only for defense, not for aggression. With the cinema, radio, and television at home, as well as chances to travel and study abroad, the members of the younger generation are becoming secular-minded. Religion plays a much less important part in their lives than it did in the lives of their parents. There is also a new spirit of tolerance, since many of the leaders are graduates of foreign schools, interested in the literature and traditions of the Christian nations.

Thirty years ago most of the philanthropies were sectarian. Today there is a conscious effort to unite representatives of different sects in various types of public service, even in connection with important enterprises like the Red Crescent and work for the Palestine refugees.

Members of different sects form not only personal friendships but also business partnerships, working together in a harmonious way. Many Christians, moreover, cooperate with their Muslim compatriots as ardent nationalists, especially in Jordan, Syria, and Lebanon.

Because of this new atmosphere of religious indifference and toleration, one might easily suppose that Islam was no longer playing an important role in connection with Arab nationalism. Nothing, however, could be further from the truth.

Islam includes at least five important elements: an intellectual dogma, a legal system, a culture, a channel for spiritual expression, and a political fraternity. It may be true that educated members of the rising generation have little interest in the ancient doctrines and laws, but it is equally certain that they still cling to the other aspects of Islam. Even though the heretical young Muslim may not hold orthodox opinions about the Qur'ān, it is such beautiful literature that he loves to hear it chanted. It is also true that one of the important features of Arab nationalism is a revival of the Arabic language and, needless to say, the basis for such a revival is the Qur'ān. Not only the sacred scriptures, but also proverbs, poetry, legends of heroes, stories like those of the *Arabian Nights,* and prayers learned in childhood are just as much a part of Arab life as Shakespeare, the classics, and the Bible are of European culture.

Elie Salem has recently written:

> The modern Arabs are increasingly emphasizing their association with Islam, and their distinct position in it. They are in fact attempting to graft the great prestige of Islam on the Arabs; and thus the nationalistic movement finds its sustenance in Islam and draws heavily on its heritage. It finds it difficult to sustain the idea of Arab nationalism without at the same time sustaining the Islamic ideal. Arab nationalism finds its intellectual stimulus in the great Arab-Islamic culture of the past—a culture which was made possible by Islam.[11]

Arabs, moreover, are highly emotional and demand some outlet for spiritual expression. Even if an educated student does not go to the mosque on Fridays or pray in the traditional way, he inevitably seeks the spiritual help that Islam provides.

In Cairo, whenever there is a formal ceremony, it begins with chanting of the Qur'ān. Then on state occasions, when the officials desire to honor some foreign guest or to celebrate some national event, the leading members of the government attend services in the Mosque of al-Azhar. Not only in Egypt, but throughout the Arab world as a whole, nationalist achievements are dignified by religious exercises of one sort or another.

At the same time that nationalism is bound to the cultural and spiritual aspects of Islam, it is also attached to the consciousness of a Muslim fraternity. In his book *Nasser of Egypt,* Wilton Wynn used the subtitle, *The Search for Dignity.* This describes what is deepest in the heart of every Arab nationalist and every Muslim. After years of exploitation and subjugation by Mamlūks and Turks, followed by European colonialism and occupation by foreign armies, Muslims as a whole and Arabs in particular wish to restore the dignity of former times. Once again they would like to be highly respected as they were in years gone by, when their ancestors gave a great culture to half the civilized world, adding to their Qur'ānic studies a revival of Greek science as well as research in mathematics, astronomy, and medicine. All Muslims of the diversified Arab states share this determination to raise both the Arabs and Islam to the dignity enjoyed during the medieval caliphate. Thus the deepest underlying emotion of nationalism and religion is one and the same. It is a desire to restore racial self-respect and to revive Islam, so that the inferiority complex of colonial days can be forgotten and Arab Muslims can hold their heads high, proud of their illustrious heritage.

Evidences of this feeling are not hard to find. After the last war, for instance, there was formed *al-Mu'tamar al-Islāmī,* or the Muslim Congress, aiming to enlist the Muslims of many lands in regaining their former positions of leadership. Four years ago, moreover, residential buildings were erected in Cairo to accommodate 4,800 foreign students. These university men enjoy scholarships so that they can study in the great Islamic center at the Mosque of al-Azhar. Mosques and centers for the teaching of Islam have been established at Paris, Washington, and other places, while Muslim missions have been sent to Indonesia, Africa, Latin America, Canada, the United States, Germany, Pakistan, India, Thailand, Japan, and other countries. At the same time a great many teachers have been supplied for schools in backward places, so as to give the youth accurate knowledge about Islam. What is significant in connection with these activities is that they have not been supported by great Muslim countries like Indonesia and Pakistan, but rather by the Arab nationalists.

The secularization, toleration, and cooperation with persons of other sects are sincere aspects of modern life. In their personal relationships, the educated young Arabs are exceedingly free from bigotry. On the other hand, no Muslim can dissociate the regaining of Arab dignity from the revival of Islam. He knows intuitively that the Arabs have never been great except when Islam was great, just as Islam itself has depended upon the Arabs for its vitality.

V. The Future

Many students of modern history wonder whether this strong attachment between religion and nationalism can continue to exist in the future. They feel that a separation is inevitable because of two important issues. The first of these is the apparent break between orthodox religion and the secular attitude of political leaders. The second issue is the choice between Communism and the West, which seems to involve either the undermining of Islam by Communist materialism or the overwhelming of Islam by so-called Christian culture and diplomacy.

Let us first discuss the problem of secularization as opposed to orthodoxy.

As each of the Arab republics has gained independence, the first concern of the leaders has been to enlighten and uplift the less fortunate classes of society. The Ottomans gave out their lands as great fiefs, allowing officials and noblemen to exploit their peasants in a brutal way. The French and British did a great deal for the upper classes of society, enabling them to become wealthy and providing them with many advantages. On the other hand, except for some praiseworthy efforts to help the peasants in Palestine and a few other places, the colonial officials neglected the rural populations.

Unlike the influential citizens of former times, the new nationalist leaders belong to the peasantry and the lower middle class. Their first concern, therefore, is to establish democratic institutions and to provide education, public health, irrigation and improved agriculture, industry, and recreation for the poor. Thus it is evident that in the future Arab nationalism is going to encourage socialism and the idea of the welfare state.

At first the orthodox Muslim scholars found it difficult to accept socialistic reforms. The Qur'ān gives full approval to the right of private ownership: "And eat not up your property among yourselves in vanity, nor seek by it to gain the hearing of the judges that ye may knowingly devour a portion of the property of others wrongfully." [12] More mature thought, however, has made the authorities feel that the Qur'ān not only prescribes the right to own private property, but also protection against an uneven distribution of wealth. Thus there is the command to pay the *zakāh,* which is a tax collected from the more fortunate members of the community, in order to give aid to the poor.[13]

This appeal for social justice is beautifully rendered in another verse of the Qur'ān:

> It is not righteousness that ye turn your faces to the East and the West; but righteous is he who believeth in Allah and the Last Day and the angels and the Scripture and the Prophets; and giveth wealth, for love of Him, to kinsfolk and to orphans and the needy and the wayfarer and to those who ask, and to set slaves free; and observeth proper worship and payeth the poor-due. And those who keep their treaty when they make one, and the patient in tribulation and adversity and the time of stress. Such are they who are sincere. Such are the God-fearing.[14]

In the light of Qur'ānic passages like those quoted, many young Muslims feel that the practical aspects of Islam are much more important than the ritual and dogma. Even the orthodox scholars, moreover, are willing to endorse the efforts of nationalist leaders to introduce socialism. In other words, they give their approval to experiments even as radical as nationalization of commercial and industrial companies, fixing of minimum wages and rents, limitation of property ownership, social security, vast housing projects, universal education, and socialized medicine—provided private ownership is respected within reasonable limits. It is, for instance, a common custom to exchange 3 per cent government bonds for property confiscated by the state. Although the Suez Canal Company was chartered as an Egyptian rather than a foreign firm, a huge indemnity was paid to the shareholders when it was nationalized.

The modification of the theory of private ownership is only one illustration of how Muslim jurists and theologians are adopting new ideas so as to give nationalist leaders the encouragement they need to make reforms. A few other examples will explain the matter further.

When I first went to Beirut in 1913, the Mufti presiding over the Muslim community was vehemently opposed to the emancipation of women, modern music, photographs and statues showing the human form, mixed dancing, and the cinema. In Egypt and other countries, reformers advocating an end of the veil were condemned as heretics. Today, even the highly respected shaykhs take their wives to the cinema, one of the Egyptian cabinet ministers is a woman, and scores of Muslim girls, often in two-piece bathing suits, enjoy the beaches at Alexandria and Beirut.

As late as 1925, Shaykh 'Alī 'Abd al-Rāziq was disciplined for writing a book in which he advocated a separation of religion and government. At the present time it is taken for granted that a modern state is administered by its government officials with as little interference as possible from religious shaykhs.

Although initially the jurists were unwilling to admit that birth control was in keeping with the Qur'ān, formal *fatwas* (legal opinions) were finally issued permitting the use of contraceptives. More recently the Egyptian government has adopted birth control as an important policy, hoping to check the population explosion.

In spite of the efforts of men like Muḥammad 'Abduh and Iqbāl, the religious leaders objected to science teaching in their schools. Even fifty years ago, physics and chemistry as well as biology and higher mathematics were regarded as secular subjects, not altogether in harmony with the Qur'ān. Accordingly, the natural sciences were not taught in the religious institutions.

At the present time the mosque universities of al-Qarawīyīn in Morocco and al-Azhar in Cairo are being transformed into great modern institutions, with the full cooperation of the shaykhs. Not only will the natural and social sciences be taught in a modern way at al-Azhar, but there will also be colleges of medicine, engineering, agriculture, and business administration.

Illustrations of this sort make it evident that religious conservatism, which formerly obstructed all types of reform, is giving way to a spirit of progress. Today, the national leaders and religious authorities of most of the Arab states are working as partners, striving to accomplish reforms long overdue. Their efforts should yield rich fruits, as illiteracy is overcome, wealth distributed, women emancipated, the national economy improved by scientific methods, and the lower classes uplifted.

At the same time that the nationalist leaders are supported by the better educated and more radical members of the rising generation, the religious chiefs are encouraging the illiterate and conservative members of the older generation to accept the new benefits being offered to them. In the future, therefore, as in the past, the progress of the Arabs seems destined to depend upon cooperation between the forces of nationalism and religion.

Even if there actually is going to be teamwork rather than friction between the orthodox shaykhs and radical government officials, there is the second question: How can Islam continue to be a force among the Arab nationalists if they are obliged to accept the supremacy either of the West or of Communism?

The issue is complicated by the fact that many members of the younger generation have become so agnostic and revolutionary that Communism seems to offer the solution to their national problems. At the same time there are large numbers of men and women who, having studied in foreign schools, believe that the Western lands have become dominant in world affairs because of social freedom, scientific research, and technological achievement. They would like to discard the ancient doctrines and social traditions of Islam which they feel have been responsible for the weakness and backwardness of the Arabs. They are convinced that their countries can rival the Christian powers in importance only if they substitute the ultramodern culture of the West for the outmoded medievalism of Islam. Although the superficial reactions of these young extremists seem to be important, they actually do not carry as much weight as the mature judgments of the experienced leaders.

The more responsible members of the reform movement realize that from the West they must derive as much knowledge as possible about science, technology, and industry. They also appreciate the importance of progressive ideas for social life, such as monogamy, coeducation, participation of women in public affairs, birth control, urban improvement, and suppression of slavery. Largely because of the radio, television, and cinema, they are becoming interested in Western music, art, and drama.

At the same time they are seeking new ideas from Russia about government ownership, public welfare, and farmers' cooperatives. They also count on Russia to help them with engineering projects and to supply them with well-trained technicians. They make a special effort to obtain military supplies, both from the Communists and the Western nations; their purpose in doing this is not to form alliances with foreign powers, but rather to strengthen their own Arab states for self-defense.

The influential Muslim nationalists, however, wish to gain these benefits from both the Communist and Western nations on condition that they can escape the evil influences of Russia and the West. They feel that life in Europe and America is too materialistic and too lacking in social restraint, their impressions of the Western world being largely based upon French and American films. They point out that the most disastrous wars in history have been caused by the European nations and they regard as scandalous the race inequality, constant strikes, and incorrigible children of America and other lands. At the same time, they fear many aspects of Communism. They especially object to the atheism in Russia and mistrust the imperialism of both Russia and China. Arabs who have visited the Muslim communities of the U.S.S.R. lament the way in which the school children are being weaned from the religion of their fathers. They also object to the lack of freedom in the Communist world, as well as to the apparent poverty of the people as a whole.

What the thoughtful leaders wish to accomplish is to avoid making a choice between Communism and the West. They are just as anxious today to defend themselves from non-Muslim domination as they were at the time of St. Louis and during the invasion of Napoleon. They are convinced that Islam should not be Western or Communist, but rather a third force in the world. Although they no longer expect Islam to be a militant theocracy, they do insist that it must be a spiritual brotherhood, universally respected and strong enough to safeguard the integrity of the Arab states and other Muslim lands.

In his recently published book, *Modern Islam: The Search for Cultural Identity,* Professor von Grunebaum has included an interesting chapter on the "Problems of Muslim Nationalism." He has also translated significant passages from numerous modern articles and books. In one place he quotes Mahjūb bin Mīlād of Tunisia as saying about his country: ". . . she is neither Eastern nor Western, but combines in splendor the purest qualities and the loftiest values of East and West, yet is independent of both whenever she feels the necessity of adhering to her deepest sentiments, her freshest thoughts, and her purest intuitions." [15]

This conception of Islam as a third world power is not a negative doctrine, but something very positive. Implying much more than neutrality, it inspires the Arabs to exert a guiding influence in many parts of Asia and Africa. Even though they do not expect to expand their political frontiers, the Arab leaders do wish to strengthen their position in world affairs by gaining the support of other neutral lands. The principal means of achieving this cooperation is Islam.

This brief survey makes it evident that from the day when the Prophet Muḥammad dismounted from his camel at al-Madīnah until our own time, Islam and Arab nationalism have been closely bound together. Because of the intellectual, social, and political revolutions of the modern world, this association is being threatened as never before in history. In spite of the tremendous changes taking place all around us, however, there is reason to believe that during the years to come religion will continue to play an important role in the drama of Arab nationalism.

NOTES

1. Qur'ān, LIII, 19, 20, 23, 31, etc.
2. Qur'ān, LXXVIII, 17–23. These verses and others that follow are quoted from the Pickthall translation.
3. Qur'ān, XCII, 12–18.
4. Qur'ān, LXI, 8–9.
5. Mirza Abū al-Fadl, *Sayings of the Prophet Muhammad* (Allahabad, 1924), p. 163.
6. al-Maqrīzī, *Kitāb al-Sulūk* (Cairo, 1956–58), Vol. 1, p. 346.
7. M. de Bourrienne, *The Life of Napoleon Bonaparte* (London, 1831), Vol. 1, p. 150.
8. *Ibid.*, p. 159.
9. Muḥammad Iqbāl, *The Reconstruction of Religious Thought in Islam* (Lahore, 1958), pp. 55, 82, 123, and 157.
10. Iqbāl Singh, *The Ardent Pilgrim* (London, 1951), p. 53.
11. "Nationalism and Islam," *Muslim World,* Vol. 52 (October, 1962), p. 282.
12. Qur'ān, II, 188.
13. Qur'ān, II, 43.
14. Qur'ān, II, 177.
15. Gustave E. von Grunebaum, *Modern Islam: The Search for Cultural Identity* (Berkeley and Los Angeles, 1962), p. 154.

Islam and the Foreign Policy of Egypt

By P. J. Vatikiotis

Introduction

Although President Nāṣir appears to be trying to replace the Islamic basis of Arab identity for Egypt with an indigenous revolutionary socialism,[1] Egypt's historical position in the Islamic world remains culturally and politically crucial for any consideration of the role of Islam in Egyptian foreign and domestic policy. Today, a revived but sharpened sense of identity with the Islamic ethos, civilization, and culture permits the rulers of Egypt to promote a politically useful Arab consciousness among the masses.

Since the end of the eleventh century, Egypt has been directly involved in the sharpest and most direct confrontations between Christian Europe and the Islamic Arab lands. After a few centuries during which the Arabs were relatively isolated from Europe—albeit there never was a total break—the confrontation between Europeans and Arabs was renewed with far-reaching impact through Egypt in 1798. Since that time, a new dimension has been given to the socio-economic and political evolution of the Arab world—a dimension which until now has been considered by most students to be directly contradictory, if not in opposition, to the Islamic nature of Arab societies.

It is not possible or practical, within the limits of one essay, to trace all the reactions and responses of Egyptians to this modern outside force over the past 150 years.[2] This essay is therefore limited to a discussion of certain phenomena relevant to the relationship between Islam and Egypt's policy toward other Arab countries.[3]

Further, the writer assumes that the use of Islam as an instrument of Egyptian foreign policy cannot be concretely documented by a chronological listing of official acts or public policy statements. A content analysis of the Egyptian press and radio is deliberately avoided, because such an analysis would be exposed to the inevitable contradictions of official and unofficial public statements about Islam and Islamic unity.

Thus, in an interview with American newsmen on March 3, 1960, President Nāṣir, commenting on the Baghdad Pact, said:

> I do not believe in mixing religion and politics. . . . What would the world be like if we had an Islamic Pact, a Jewish Pact, a Buddhist Pact? I do not think that such pacts would make the world wonderful. Peoples of different creeds would not thereby be able to live together. Although Pakistan is an Islamic coun-

try, and the U.A.R. is an Islamic country, I cannot find anything in this to justify the conclusion of a military pact between the two countries.[4]

Yet the following month, in Lahore, he devoted his entire speech before the Anjuman Himayat-i-Islam society to the value of Islamic teachings and to the community of spirit that exists between Pakistan and the U.A.R.[5] In his press conference at Lahore on April 14, 1960, when asked whether he favored the creation of a Muslim bloc, Nāṣir replied that "an association of nations on the basis of religion would give one to fanaticism and would not aid world peace. Minorities, moreover, would suffer as a result." [6] But two days later, at the end of his visit to Pakistan, Nāṣir emphasized, in a joint communiqué with Ayub Khan, that the friendship and co-operation between the two countries was inspired by the Islamic bonds of brotherhood which united the two nations.[7] Later in the same year, in a speech welcoming Ayub Khan to Egypt, Nāṣir explained Pakistan's nonrecognition of Israel as having been determined by the "urge of Islamic comradeship felt by Pakistan." [8]

No clear role for Islam in Egyptian foreign policy can be elicited from such statements. Thus, in February–April, 1959, the Egyptian press and radio ascribed Egypt's differences with Iraq to Islamic values—Islam versus atheistic Communism, and Islamic solidarity versus sectarian fragmentation of the *ummah,* or community of the faithful. And since May, 1962, a distinction between the true Islam, "the religion of justice and equality," and the deviationist Islam of "corruption, reaction, exploitation, and tyranny" has been promoted and publicized by all Egyptian mass media, as well as by President Nāṣir himself. This distinction was made in order to exclude the so-called reactionary regimes of Saudi Arabia, the Yemen of the Imāms Aḥmad and Badr, and the Hashimite Kingdom of Jordan from the pale of the "religion of Islam"

—a religion synonymous with a "revolution which first laid down the socialist principles of justice and equality." [9] The results of this deliberate differentiation of Islam—between Egypt, representing radical nationalism and "Arab socialism" on the one hand, and Saudi Arabia and Jordan (and the Yemen until September, 1962), representing backward anti-Islamic autocracy and tribalism on the other—is too well known to outline in detail here.

Although the role of Islam in Egyptian foreign policy cannot emerge clearly from an examination of public pronouncements by state officials and other political leaders, it would be hasty and injudicious to conclude that Islam has no place in Egyptian policy orientation and policy formation. In fact, a further premise of this essay is that there is a significant and fundamental relationship between Egyptian policy and Islam, especially in the complex area of ideology —in the formulation and reformulation of social and political goals and values for modern Egypt, and in the Nāṣir regime's conception of Arab nationalism and the unity of the Arab countries. The subtle involvement of Islam will be found in recent Egyptian ideological considerations about Arab socialism and the requisites of revolution. In the course of the essay that follows, this kind of relationship between Islam and Egyptian policy—especially in the period since July, 1961 —is examined briefly and placed in historical perspective. Such an examination enables us to assess the use of Islam as an instrument of Egyptian policy—particularly the role of the religious institutions,[10] represented by the Azhar Mosque and University, in the mobilization and effective utilization of a religion-sanctioned political program that can serve a so-called "revolutionary Arab socialist policy" of liberation, industrialization, and modernization.

In this connection, it is suggested that all three variants of Islamic consciousness—solidarity, religious reform, and socio-political activities—are involved in Egypt's recent bid—at least as expressed since May, 1962, in Nāṣir's National Charter—to pre-empt the leadership of an emerging modern and socialist "Arab nation." Implicit, also, in this discussion, is the view that the revolutionary ideology and policy of radical reform in Egypt, as well as Egypt's policy against reactionary conservative regimes in some of the Arab states, are not really at variance with Islamic religious practices. To this extent, an intense preoccupation with the alleged conflict between religion and policy (or politics) would be unjustified and futile. At the same time, the incompatibility between Islam and nationalism assumed by students in the past becomes an academic myth (although it is theoretically tenable)—for one may agree that the religious institution, which, according to Sir Hamilton Gibb, was characteristically separate from the political institution,[11] has lost the kind of independent influence it used to exert, say, in Mamlūk or Ottoman Egypt, and has now come under the more direct and total control of the ruling establishment. Thus, it is now mobilized, or called upon, both to intellectualize and to popularize the revolutionary nature of Islam, its socialist principles, and its modernizing force. To be sure, it continues to check many proclivities on the part of the political institution to further secularize Arab society or to recast its sociopolitical values on the basis of an ideology free of Islam, its tenets, or virtues. To this extent, religious leaders may exert a certain amount of influence over the rulers. But the objective of the state's policy is not hindered by such influence; on the contrary, in the pursuit of its political goals, the state tends to orient in its favor the men and institutions of religion by allocating new tasks to them. The state has thus been able to win the support of religious leaders and organizations, which, in turn, have recently tried to present the Egyptian revolutionary regime to the rest of the Muslim Arabs as the model of regenerated Islam and the harbinger of another Islamic Golden Age.[12]

More controversial, perhaps, is the suggestion that the belief and national-myth infrastructure of the political community, which Egyptian policy seeks to establish both in Egypt and in the other Arab countries, necessarily antedates secular nationalism. Realizing the mistake of earlier liberal nationalists who attempted to undermine and displace the prenationalist Islamic ethos with a purely secular conception of nationalism, the present Egyptian regime is careful to avoid committing the same error in its search for a formula and basis of solidarity. The principles of its revolutionary Arab socialism are carefully linked to those of prenationalist ideological structures. Thus, Islam-sanctioned revolutionary nationalism—even socialism—serves to assimilate politically individuals and groups who for a long time have identified themselves with groups lesser than the state or nation, let alone an Arab nation. Thus, Islam-based revolutionary nationalism and socialism can more readily achieve the equation of the nation with the state and supersede all other group loyalties. The totalitarian nature of nationalism's demand for allegiance is more easily achieved when such nationalism derives from, or is inspired by, the value system of a religion which for over 1,300 years has regulated the social, political, and cultural relations of individuals and states. One might even suggest, first, that there can be no purely secular Arab nationalism in Egypt, and, second, that secular nationalism is not really necessary for the attainment of modernity—a concept and condition that are until now essentially Western-inspired.[13] In this case, however, modernity does not presuppose or prescribe a democratic polity.

Besides the historical and legal background of Islam's inevitable involvement in Arab politics—and in this case, in contemporary Egyptian policy—the Arabs' own preoccupation with their identity with Islam, both as a religion and a civilization—a heritage, if you will—renders it a major source, if not *the* source, of their national consciousness, centering upon the Prophet Muḥammad and the Holy Qur'ān. One may ask, "What about pre-Islamic Arab consciousness?" The question is irrelevant, because modern Arabs think in terms of a political consciousness that is directly identified with the political, military, and imperial success of Islam, and, more simply, the relation of this success to the spread of the Islamic message. Thus, although the first political success of the Arabs on a mass scale was achieved under the banner of Islam, Egyptians and other modern Arabs began their national regeneration by questioning the strength of the Islamic community vis-à-vis outside forces, before they could awaken any feeling for an Arab nation. The theory (which, we shall argue, holds for Egyptian policy today) was developed that the political or national decline of the Arabs was inexorably connected with the decline of Islamic power. In this sense, Islam came to form the core of Arab national ideology—a point of view accepted by apologists for Islam—particularly the fundamentalists and conservatives among them. Their argument, briefly, was that Islam minutely defined the relations between man and God, man and the state, man and man; that it set up a system of values and virtues whose attainment and maintenance constituted the Islamic ideal state and society. Arab national strength declined with the deviation and unwillingness, or inability, of Muslims to strive for the attainment of this Islamic ideal. Instead, they strove for the attainment of an ideal imported from Europe. This, according to Islamic nationalists, was a mistake.

The Egyptian regime accepts these premises, but without the apology or the fundamentalism. It merely starts with the assertion of a special and privileged position of the Arab in the Islamic nexus. In this privileged position, the Arab is duty-bound to effect the modernization of Islam, which modernization, in turn, is measured by socioeconomic and political advancement.

The first political feelings of solidarity along modern nationalist lines were mixed with an Islamic aversion to control by infidels. Somewhat later, there was an attempt to exclude the Islamic element from the level of political organization, administration, legislation, and economic activity, in order to produce the machinery required for a viable modern state. This practical exclusion of religion from state functions not only has been accepted by many Arabs but continues unimpeded. What the Egyptian regime has revived is the earlier conception of Arab Islamic solidarity in order to activate the desire for independence, revolution, and modernization. In doing so, it has also found it necessary to reinterpret the role of the Arabs in Islam, as well as to reinterpret the socioeconomic and political meaning of Islam itself. This reinterpretation of the role of Islam in the so-called new Egyptian (or Arab socialist) society, which is allegedly desired by all Arab revolutionaries and progressives, becomes the arena of conflict with those who are opposed to this society.[14]

An outline of the phases of Islamic reform in Egypt since 1870 will serve to illustrate these trends. Jamāl al-Dīn al-Afghānī brought to Egypt the call for Islamic solidarity, strength, and unity with a view to opposing the encroachments of Europe. His legacy was one of active agitation for a stronger and united Islamic world. His disciple Muḥammad 'Abduh settled for a quiet evolutionary and rationalist reform of Islam (i.e., one within the strict rules of the theological discipline), in an attempt, first, to reconcile the faith (or revelation) with reason—the basis for reform and modernization—and, second, to educate the members of the Islamic community in such a way as to provide them with a responsible ethic or theory of action. 'Abduh's disciple, Rashīd Rida, and his *Salafīyah* movement, with its theologically more systematic, albeit apologetic and therefore less positive, endeavor, represented a return to the practices of the orthodox religious doctors and a possible reinstitution of the caliphate. The ideas put forward by 'Abduh—that evolutionary reforms in theology, the educational institutions of al-Azhar, and the *Sharī'ah* judiciary would gradually educate the Muslims and liberate their society from its backwardness and difficulties—were by the 1930's rejected in favor of more activist, authoritarian, and less theoretical Islamic nationalist tendencies [15]—a sort of a return to Afghānī's activism, but with a serious difference. The activism now would apply specifically to the Arabs, as the "best" (*al-afḍal*) in Islam, and would not seek a fundamentalist puritan return to the past, as did the Wahhabī movement, for instance. This trend can perhaps explain the recent concentrated interest of Egyptian and other Arab authors in the Syrian 'Abd al-Raḥmān al-Kawākibī. The latter was very conscious of the weakness of the political community, which to him was synonymous with the *ummah,* or the religious community. But he was not disturbed by the weakness of the Ottoman state, only by the weakness of the Arabs, for they had the first role in Islam.[16] He was seeking to establish Islamic leadership for the Arabs to the exclusion of other Muslims. This was also a goal of later Islamic nationalists, including the Muslim Brethren in Egypt, of theorists of Islamic nationalism such as 'Abd al-Raḥmān al-Bazzāz, and of Islamic leaders in Egypt such as Aḥmad Fū'ād al-Ahwānī, Muḥammad al-Bahī, and Shaykh Maḥmūd Shalṭūṭ, Rector of al-Azhar.[17]

Finally, before proceeding with our analysis, it may be noted that Egyptian policy apparently does not aim at the establishment of an Islamic state in Egypt or of an Islamic Arab empire in the traditional-legal sense of these terms. We should not conclude, however, that the Egyptian rulers are not actively interested in the sense of pride and feeling of solidarity that a successful revolutionary integration of the Arabs under Egyptian leadership can engender with the aid of Islam. This Egyptian model for revolution properly steeped in Islamic virtue (provided Islam is carefully accommodated to the prevailing sociopolitical conditions when necessary) becomes that much more appealing and alluring. As Nāṣir himself told the Preparatory Committee of the Congress of Popular Forces in 1962, "Egypt has no choice but to be Arab. . . . Arab Egypt's struggle for Arab unity is a historical responsibility, shouldered by the Egyptian people as per their capabilities and resources." And in countering other Muslims' attacks upon his socialism—namely, those of Radio Mecca—Nāṣir, addressing the same Committee, said: "They have forgotten that the religion [Islam] is the religion of justice and equality. . . . Religion is against social tyranny; against exploitation in all its aspects. The Islamic religion was the first revolution which established the principles of socialism, and these pertain to equality and justice." [18]

Sir Hamilton Gibb has argued that a significant effect of the abolition of the Ottoman Caliphate in 1924 was a tendency among some Arabs to work for a revival of Mahdism, which would forcefully integrate the Islamic world.[19] Although Egypt's policy favors an eclectic but tactical use of neo-Mahdism, Nāṣir's regime combines the establishment of a just and equitable Islamic realm in the Arab lands with socialism and the requisites of a modern industrialized state. The radical revolutionary aspect of the regime is no departure from Mahdism, since the latter is by definition revolutionary in nature.

I

The abolition of the caliphate by Kemāl Atatürk in 1924—indeed, the dismantling of the Islamic edifice in Turkey by the disestablishment of the *Sharī'ah*—had strong repercussions among Egyptians. Their concern for its fate preoccupied them for at least three years, and involved not only al-Azhar and the *'ulamā'*, but also the Palace, Parliament, and other Arab rulers.[20] This Egyptian attitude was inevitable considering the pre-eminent position of al-Azhar and Cairo in the world of Islamic learning, as centers for the propagation and defense of the faith. The upholders of Islamic tradition represented in al-Azhar and its related organizations obviously were shocked by the abrupt, forceful disposal of Islamic institutions. At the same time, Western-trained intellectuals became involved in a debate about the fundamental nature and necessity of such institutions.[21] The attack upon Islam was massive, but the defense was no less vociferous. Egyptians once again declared their national concern with the problems of the Islamic faith and community. One may argue that today, however, there is no concern over such matters as the caliphate; that Egyptians actually have led in weakening the bases of Islamic institutions by abolishing the *Sharī'ah* or religious courts, by curtailing the vast activities of traditional religious orders (*Tarīqat*), and by introducing modern secular-inspired reforms in the very seat of Islamic learning and culture—al-Azhar and its related organizations. How can we then argue for a significant relationship between Islam and Egyptian policy today?

The performance of the military regime since 1952 indicates that a revolutionary group of nationalist leaders (the "Free Officers") is conscious of (1) the importance and efficacy of the Islamic link between their goals and the mobilization of the community for their achievement; (2) the necessity of resuming the efforts of Muslims to reform their religious and traditional institutions to meet the requirements of a modern age; and (3) the natural and useful connection between religious belief and political duty, insofar as this connection can inspire and invigorate political performance for the attainment of the new leadership's objectives at home and abroad.

The first dimension of the Free Officers' political orientation became apparent early in their rule. The destruction in 1954 of their political rivals and enemies, the Muslim Brethren, did not result in a sweeping attack upon all forms of religious activity, institutions, or thought. Instead, the ruling junta iterated their respect for, and adherence to, the Islamic faith and culture, culminating in the establishment of the Islamic Congress in November, 1954.[22] The events of 1955—the Israeli raid on Gaza, the formation of the Baghdad Pact, and the Egyptian-Czech arms deal—further pushed the Egyptian leaders into an Arab-Islamic frame of political orientation—and particularly articulation—culminating in rigorous and systematic use of the religious sermon (*khuṭbah*) for political purposes. The pulpit of the mosque became once again, as in earlier times, the platform for communication from the leader to the public.[23] The Suez Crisis of 1956 further accentuated the feeling of infidel attack upon Islam, and Egyptian leaders sought to acquire the heroic aura of Saladin.

The other two dimensions of Egyptian policy orientation are only now becoming clear. They can best be traced through a discussion of, first, the National Charter of May, 1962, and its importance to both Egypt and the larger Arab-Islamic community; second, the renewed importance of al-Azhar, as indicated by the latest Reform and Reorganization Law of June, 1961; and third, the marked concern of writers and intellectuals with establishing a basically Arab-Islamic political legacy for Egypt.

II

However one may assess the record of Nāṣir's regime over the past ten years, one must recognize that since July, 1961, it has come forward with recommendations at home (and declarations abroad) that, theoretically at least, indicate serious revolutionary intentions. It is not improper, therefore, to consider their importance for Egyptians at home and their possible impact on the other Arab countries. That Egypt puts forth her claim to lead the modernization of Arab societies in the Middle East was made clear on May 21, 1962, in President Nāṣir's Charter to the Egyptian people. Briefly, the Charter proposes a political program for Egypt's "Second Revolution," [24] initiated by the promulgation of socialist measures in July, 1961. Here, however, we are more concerned with those proposals of the Charter that relate to Egypt's aspiration to Arab leadership in terms of leading Arab society to modernity and the Arab peoples to unity. We are also concerned with the relation between Islam as defined in our introductory remarks and this desired Arab leadership.

The Charter recognizes the inadequacy of the traditional (as distinguished from the reinterpreted) Islamic ethic for the advancement of Arab society. It proposes that social change must be radical; that the enemy of the "Arab nation" is no longer imperialism in its naked form of direct control, but disguised through local reactionaries. The "socialist revolution" in Egypt is now the principal weapon against "reaction" (as Nāṣir said on December 23, 1961); [25] Cairo is the center of social revolution for the whole Middle East. Egyptian socialism will emerge victorious from the battle against reaction to lead in unifying the Arab world and liberating it from capitalist exploitation and imperialist domination.

In the Second Revolution the struggle for Arabism (i.e., Pan-Arabism) is identified with the struggle for socialism, and Nāṣir now becomes the champion of social reform and, as we shall see, of Islam-sanctioned social reform. Egypt is seen as the *avant garde* of the Arab struggle, the base of Arab unity and of a progressive Islamic community; those who are opposed to Egypt's new socialism are really against any progress in the Arab world *and* against the strengthening of Islamic society. The Second Revolution will build an economically, socially, and politically strong Egypt—a model of national endeavor to be emulated and a pioneer in Arab development. Egypt will also represent a reforming and modernizing Islam, whereas rulers like King Ḥusayn of Jordan and King Sa'ūd of Arabia represent stagnating and reactionary Islam. The Charter, moreover, does not stop at the distinction between two types of Arab governments—progressive, led by Egypt, on the one hand, and reactionary on the other—but argues that it is incumbent upon the people to defeat the latter, preferably with Egyptian help. "The U.A.R., firmly convinced that she is an integral part of the Arab Nation, must propagate her call for unity and the principles it embodies, so that it should be at the disposal of every Arab citizen, without hesitating for one minute before the outworn argument that this would be considered an interference in the affairs of others."[26] Apart from the obvious implications of this statement, the Charter suggests the existence of "Arab citizens" as distinguished from the citizens of the various independent Arab states.

Egypt's choice to lead the Arab countries and unite them by socialist example is, on the surface, a plausible one. That Egypt offers the most successful revolution, so far, against the previous generation of Arab leadership, is undeniable. That the regime in Egypt has broken the power of landowning pashas is also a valid claim. That it has survived foreign invasion is proudly proclaimed. At the same time, the capital city Cairo—with its Azhar University (seat of Islamic learning *par excellence* for a thousand years), its secular state universities, mass communication media (radio, television, press, cinema), and its literary and publishing activity—renders Egypt easily the most advanced Arabic-speaking Muslim country today. It is on these bases that Nāṣir's regime came forward in 1962 to reiterate boldly that an Arab nation really exists: It stretches from Morocco in the west to the Arabian (Persian) Gulf in the east. What makes the Arabs one nation, according to Nāṣir, is (1) their recent experience of freedom from foreign domination, (2) their desire to accede to modernity with all its emblems of economic and social well-being, (3) their aspiration to strength and unity, and (4) their

Islamic faith. The fact that disparities in development exist among them is only a phase in the revolutionary process that now grips the entire Arab world; those that are not independent will soon become so; those under archaic political regimes will achieve more radical political arrangements. What this implies is that the ideal is no longer a mere weapon against outsiders; it has been turned inward against a certain class of Arab political leaders. Egyptian political leaders now argue that to be a loyal Arab one must be a progressive socialist. If, then, as Islamic leaders in Egypt have recently opined, to be a good Muslim an Arab must also be a socialist, one can argue that it is a duty of all good Muslims to render the community of the faithful socialist and, thus, progressive. Although it is difficult to elicit a secular nationalism from the Islamic base, it is not unreasonable to expect that the rectification of the Islamic community along socialist lines becomes an extension of the moral duty of all "Arab citizens" in the Egyptian definition. The eradication of "unprogressive" regimes by the "progressive" elements is thus no longer immoral, and constitutes neither illegal subversion nor heretical internecine warfare among coreligionists.

If the preceding briefly, yet fairly, represents what the Charter envisages as the role and destiny of Egypt—namely, to be the first Arab nationalist, revolutionary, and progressive socialist society and political system in the Arab Middle East—it also sets up Egypt as the model for revolution throughout the Arab countries. Our earlier reference to the nature and objectives of such revolution indicates a vigorously novel departure from traditional Islam. This may well turn out to be the case. But it has already been argued that the revolutionary regime has not been, and is not now, willing to declare a total detachment from Islam; on the contrary, it is anxious to carry Islam forward with it. We must, therefore, turn now to a consideration of one of the methods being used to do this, and suggest in conclusion that such an alliance with Islam is, for the time being, necessary for Egypt's Arab policy.

Our case study will deal with the efforts of al-Azhar and religious leaders, as well as of some Egyptian intellectuals, to attune a reformed and activated Islam to the requirements of Egypt's bid for the progressive leadership of all the Arabs. At the same time, we shall try to show that the political establishment welcomes this support from the recognized center of religious education, for it considers it effective both at home and abroad.

III

Early attempts by Egyptian nationalist leaders to motivate Egyptian society toward the attainment of modern national goals necessarily included a desire to reform the religious institutions, especially if the dichotomy between secular and religious education were not to continue. The great Shaykh Muḥammad 'Abduh sought earnestly to reform al-Azhar. Many of his followers, especially members of the Ummah Party, and others since 1911, succeeded in getting the Egyptian Government to enact a series of reform measures to meet this problem. Shaykhs such as al-Ẓawāhirī, Muṣṭafā 'Abd al-Rāziq, and al-Marāghī attempted in one way or another to push al-Azhar into the stream of modern society.[27] It was not until June 23, 1961, that the Egyptian Government decreed the most radical and sweeping reform measure affecting al-Azhar and all of its institutions. Law No. 103/1961 is epochal not only in its aim to revolutionize the whole character of religious education, but more so for its possible effects upon society as a whole and its impact among Arabs everywhere. The exciting potential of its success may have permanent repercussions in the Arab countries and in all Islamic societies.[28]

Bearing in mind our original premise that the regime in

Egypt is consciously and deliberately seeking to associate its revolution and its objectives with a reinterpreted Islamic nexus, two initial questions may be asked regarding the importance of al-Azhar in this connection. First, what is the Azharite reaction and response to the law of June, 1961? Second, what is the Azharite view of Nāṣir's Charter for National Action presented on May 21, 1962? Since it is impossible to deal with these two questions by a complete perusal of all Azharite expressions over the past two years, we shall confine ourselves to statements by leading Azharites, such as Shaykh Shalṭūṭ, Shaykh of al-Azhar; Dr. Muḥammad al-Bahī, until recently Chancellor of al-Azhar University; and Aḥmad Ḥasan al-Zayyāt, Editor of *Majallat al-Azhar* (*Journal of the Azhar*).

Basically, Law No. 103/1961 (to reorganize al-Azhar and its affiliated institutions as justified in the Explanatory Memorandum of Minister of State Kamāl al-Dīn Maḥmūd Rif'at), first concedes the central importance of al-Azhar for the continuance of the nation's religious and cultural personality. Second, it emphasizes the importance of modern-trained Azhar graduates who will contribute to the welfare of the Arab nation by recommending "a reform movement to bring al-Azhar closer to the modern age, while retaining its special characteristics and values for the preservation of the faith and the protection of the Islamic heritage." Third, the government sees no contradiction in reorganizing al-Azhar as a modern institution of higher learning, because "Islam in its true meaning does not distinguish between religious and secular knowledge. It is a social religion which regulates the conduct of man in life. . . . Every Muslim must be a man of religion and of the world at one and the same time." Fourth, by training the man of religion to earn his livelihood in modern professional and technical vocations, Egypt will ensure that no Azharite would be isolated from his fellow-citizens in a modern industrialized society. Thus, the importance of renovating al-Azhar lies in the recognition of its central place and contribution to the achievement of the goals of the Egyptian revolution.

According to the Minister, previous attempts at reforming al-Azhar were superficial. In the past, al-Azhar itself was forced into rigid, backward conservatism because it had to defend Islam against foreign attack. Imperialism tried to promote a dichotomy between the Islamic heritage and modern life. Now, while al-Azhar must remain basically the largest single Islamic institution in the world, it must also be in a position to elevate and revive Islam by expanding the scope of knowledge. In this manner, al-Azhar will produce religious leaders who combine practical and scientific training with their religious mission. Religion will no longer be their only profession. Finally, when al-Azhar takes its proper place in the work of building a new society, the old barriers between al-Azhar as the "fortress of Islam" and the rest of the Muslims will come tumbling down.

The most radical departure from Azharite tradition proposed by the Reorganization Law is the introduction of four modern colleges: Government and Public Administration, Industry and Engineering, Agriculture, and Medicine. These are added to the original colleges of Sacred Law, Theology, and Arabic Studies. The importance of al-Azhar's work in Arab and non-Arab Islamic countries is reflected in the establishment of an Academy for Islamic Research and a Department of Islamic Education and Missions under the jurisdiction of the Higher Council of the University, headed by the Shaykh of al-Azhar.[29]

The reorganization of al-Azhar is obviously designed to bring the Azharite closer to the political elite by introducing him to modern education and by allocating to him specific tasks of national and international importance not necessarily at variance with his Islamic belief and sentiment. The regime therefore argues that al-Azhar must be strengthened in order to lead in the liberation of the Islamic community, and thus to remain, as always, the "fortress of religion and Arabism." The political significance of this measure can be appreciated from the fact that the reorganized Azhar will be independent of the state university system, which is normally under the direction of the Ministry of Education. Instead, over-all supervision of al-Azhar's affairs is entrusted to the Presidency of the Republic.[30]

Al-Azhar has a primary role in the communication between Egypt and the rest of the Arab and Muslim world and as the leading Muslim interpreter of the Egyptian revolution and its aims. "Our Cultural Centers in Benghazi, Tripoli, Rabat, Omdurman, Accra, the Philippines, Afghanistan, the U.S.A., Germany, Austria, Italy, Switzerland, Spain, Lebanon, Morocco, Pakistan, India, Indonesia, China, and other cities of the world, radiate the light of our civilization and culture until it covers all the corners of the universe." [31] The message of the Egyptian revolution which the learned men of religion explain and spread throughout the Muslim Arab countries is merely a continuation of Muḥammad's mission fourteen centuries ago.

> We Muslims possess a glorious revolution proclaimed 14 centuries ago, in order to restore to humanity its human sentiment and dignity, and to give man his proper due. He [Muḥammad] proclaimed his revolution to destroy despotism and to realize the high principles of God, namely, security and honour. This most grandiose of revolutions included many dimensions: a scientific revolution (*Iqrā' fī ismillah al-khāliq*), a social revolution with which all men become equal before God, distinguished only by piety, and a spiritual revolution in the direct relationship between God and man. . . . In the face of a world in conflict our answer must be: to return to our Islamic revolution proclaimed by the Prophet in 622, to inspire us by its scientific, moral, and spiritual import.[32]

If we can accept the argument that the Egyptian regime considers a modernized and revitalized Azhar essential to the success of its revolutionary policy at home and the propagation of its liberating message for the Arabs abroad, how does al-Azhar itself view this politically allocated task? To put the question differently, how does al-Azhar as the accepted interpreter of Islam for Egypt, and the respected religious opinion-maker for the wider Islamic community, consider the regime's concept of revolution, socialism, and Arab unity? Briefly, according to the Azharites, their role is to revive the socialism that is present in the original Islamic message and turn its meaning today into a national belief. Hence, the reorganization of al-Azhar is "one of the greatest revolutionary works, and will have a great influence on society and the other Islamic and Arabic nations." [33]

Officially, at least, the Azhar hierarchy views Nāṣir's revolution, especially the Second Revolution—beginning in July, 1961, and including the National Charter—as the start of a new era. The revolution has brought al-Azhar back to its original role in the propagation of the Islamic message and the building of an Arab society "whose principles were laid down in the Charter upon the firm bases of religion, character, knowledge, work, justice, and sufficiency in freedom, peace, and unity." [34] Al-Azhar welcomes the revolution because "revolution is of its nature, and socialism of its spirit." It further accepts the new Arab socialist order decreed by the revolution "as the whole accepts its parts . . . and because the mission of Muhammad cannot deny just socialism, for it was his message which rendered the poor his due of the rich man's wealth." [35] Nāṣir's Charter, which the people have vowed to fulfill, consists of "words from God, which were not expressed by anyone before him in the old days or today, in the West or the East, namely, that what the tormented and oppressed on earth desire they have found in the Charter." The Islamic message is not dead; the Charter has recaptured the light of Islam from "Omar in Medina to the kingship of Muawia [Mu'āwīyah] in Damascus, from the Empire of Rashīd in Baghdad to the Republic of Nasser in Cairo." [36] The National Charter is therefore a gift from God, the renewed call to God via Nāṣir.

Maḥmūd Shalṭūṭ, Shaykh of al-Azhar, is a good example of the Islamic propagandist for Nāṣir's revolution and for the Egyptian model of Arab nationalism and socialism. He has urged Arab-Islamic societies to disengage themselves from a declining and degenerate West on the one hand and an arrogant East on the other. He counsels them to return to the real "national personality" given to them by God in His Islamic message. This return will lead to unity among them, since their disunity was in great measure due to their earlier mistaken adoption of a foreign personality.[37] Concerning the unity of the Arab nation, Shalṭūṭ has both written and voiced (in broadcasts) statements consonant with official Egyptian policy and coincidental with specific acts of policy. Thus, since the Azhar Reorganization Law, the so-called Socialist Laws of July, 1961, and the proclamation of the Charter by Nāṣir, Shalṭūṭ has tried to underscore the Islamic basis of unity and the deviant nature of oppression and exploitation.[38] Lest "they burn in hell," he warns believers not to aid the tyrants—those who have not established equality between ruler and subject and who perpetuate class distinctions in Arab society. This view not only coincides with the political leadership's identification of Arab tyrants and exploiters on the Voice of the Arabs Radio and in Cairo's newspapers, but also reflects the religious leadership's blessing of the proposed socialistic aims of the Charter. "In the month of Ramaḍān, when Muslims submit to the teachings of God and His Guidance, He orders them to be one nation which does not know conflict and division." [39]

Islam, according to Shaykh Shalṭūṭ, decreed the idea of social cooperation among the members of the *ummah*. So far (i.e., before Nāṣir's revolution), the basic shortcoming of Arab Islamic states has been the exploitation of the needy. The revolution has come now to repeat the chastisement of "oppressive capitalism," which, in Shalṭūṭ's conception, includes the following vices: the extension of the power of the rich by their exploitation of the poor; the contravention of the Islamic "popular formula" which commands mutual aid in society; the undermining of belief; the corruption of society by the extended control of the materialist spirit and mentality; the prevalence of fear among all social classes; and the increase of crime. What the revolution proposes to accomplish through its Charter both in Egypt and elsewhere in the Arab lands is really similar to what Islam came to accomplish against the oppressive capitalism of Mecca—namely, to combat this "oppressive capitalism" through the *Sharī'ah,* which sanctions social cooperation and prohibits all kinds of material exploitation of one group of people by another.[40] From this one may assume that in his capacity as Shaykh of al-Azhar, Shalṭūṭ is not only informing Muslims everywhere that the socialist revolution intended by Egypt is not at variance with the faith, but—more significantly for Egyptian foreign policy—that it is a continuation of the sacred mission of Islam itself. At the same time, he is warning Muslim Arabs that it is un-Islamic and sinful to permit the existence among them of what Egypt identifies as tyrannical and exploiting regimes.[41]

Another interesting aspect of Shalṭūṭ's work in the service of Egyptian policy pertains to his conception of the role of al-Azhar after the reorganization. "Indeed, al-Azhar is the spirit of both the Arab and Muslim life; it is also a positive factor in their progress and development." [42] He asserts that Egypt's position as leader of all Muslims is not a result of progress imposed from outside but rather of al-Azhar's uninterrupted work and fame. Al-Azhar is the protector of both Islam and Arabism. "By promulgating the new law, the

U.A.R. government is aiming at making al-Azhar—as it was 1,000 years ago—the stronghold of the *religion of Arabism*. It wants Islam to be revived." [43]

One may well ask if Shalṭūṭ is not reading too much into the intentions of Egypt's political leaders. Do they, in fact, want Islam to be revived? Or do they merely want to assimilate its institutions and leadership into the policy apparatus of their proposed revolution? The latter possibility has been obvious for some time now. The revival of Islam, however, presents serious problems. First, what kind of Islam will it be, and second, what kind of a revival is planned? Our original thesis stressed the idea that the Egyptian leaders are now committed to a systematic accommodation of Islam to political reality that can also be used to buttress their revolutionary ideology and its export to the Arabs outside Egypt. The Azharites, on the other hand, seem on the surface to assume that Nāṣir and his regime are interested in restoring the eminent position of the religious institutions in the councils of the state. This assumption may be exaggerated and overenthusiastic. Nevertheless, the present Azharite leadership is encouraged to view Nāṣir as the leader who will elevate and extend Islamic power, for they see Islam as a force that will soon influence the modern world and possibly counteract Communism in Africa and Asia.[44]

Aḥmad Ḥasan al-Zayyāt, Editor of the *Azhar Journal*, is perhaps the most extreme of the Azharites in his assumption that the Nāṣir revolution will become synonymous with (1) the redemption of Muslim Arab society and (2) the restoration of Islamic power and glory. In an open letter addressed to President Nāṣir on the occasion of the Festival of Education, al-Zayyāt declared that after a long period of stagnation,

> God has willed that the Arabs should have a fourth Golden Age, to surpass the brilliance of the three previous ones. And

> so has appeared your age, Mr. President, in which . . . have been applied the principles of Islam. These were understood and believed in earlier periods but never applied. In your age government is by consultation, wealth is shared, people are equal, and they are the source of political power.[45]

He thus singles out Nāṣir as a man with a mission (*dhu risālah*), whose message for the unity of the Arabs radiates from his Charter.

A more consistent and systematic attempt to present the Charter and its socialism as basically Muslim developments in Egypt and desirable models for political action by other Arabs has come from the pen of Muḥammad al-Bahī, one-time Chancellor of al-Azhar University. A primarily conservative Islamic writer, al-Bahī has, since 1957, argued for a course in Egyptian policy that would permit the centering of the Egyptian revolution on "the tenets and virtues" of Islam. In doing so, he has not refrained from attacking the secularist modernists who would work for a totally new ethic deriving from the existential characteristics of an industrial and technological society.[46] Briefly, al-Bahī has insisted that Arab socialism is no more than a reiteration of Islamic values. If it also aims at the betterment of Egyptian and Arab society through productive work that combines material with spiritual power, the Charter becomes "a covenant on ourselves to be believers in God, in ourselves and our humanity in the Great Arab Homeland in which we live." [47]

Al-Bahī equates the central Islamic belief in one God with the socialist belief in human values of justice, cooperation, and unity, so that the message of a reorganized Azhar becomes simply one of reviving these human values. Then, to the questions of what is the socialist society and what is the role of al-Azhar in it, al-Bahī gives what he considers to be Islamic answers. Socialism, he asserts, is no more than the "solidarity and unity of a people in order to prevent the demolition of human dignity at any moment by means of the misuse of fortune, which surely leads to slavery or to social injustice . . . to realize equilibrium in society and cover the needs of the needy. Surely such a society will be a cooperative and united one." [48] Socialism is thus synonymous with humanism, and, even if the new revolutionary society will not be an Islamic one in the traditional sense, it will at least be one that revives "the conditions that Islam has called people to since its advent"—i.e., a society in which social injustice has been removed. To this extent, Arab socialism will be based on the religion, because Islam is the source of its human values. The attitude of al-Azhar, therefore—to both the Charter and the Reorganization Law decreed by the political leaders of the revolution—must be one that considers it a duty to call people to the society contemplated by the revolution. Al-Bahī even argues that Nāṣir was prompted to decree Law No. 103/1961 by his appreciation of the central role which al-Azhar can play in building this new Arab socialist society.[49]

Still more revealing is the view in Azharite literature of President Nāṣir as a revolutionary leader. This view is significant because of its circulation among Muslims outside Egypt. The most consistent picture is that of Nāṣir as the "natural leader" to whom the people have entrusted the task of re-establishing the true religious base of the Arab nation.[50] Al-Zayyāt claims that as far back as 1935, while editing another journal, *al-Risālah,* he prophesied Nāṣir's "coming." Nāṣir has come, like the Mahdī, to stamp out corruption and tyranny. His fierce call to social justice and Arab socialism has reverberated throughout the Arab world and especially the Arabian Peninsula, as has been evident in the Yemen recently.[51] The new revolutionary society Nāṣir proposed in his Charter is in accordance with the spirit of the sacred law, because, "according to the nature of the message of the Islamic religion, God promulgated it a socialist one." Thus, the July, 1961, laws derive from "our cultural heritage and our merciful sacred law, as well as from the nature of our peaceful Arab people." [52]

One can also deduce from the writings of the Azharites that the Arab socialist revolution can be led only by a "naturally selected leader" (Nāṣir), a head of state, in whom people confide and to whom they give their oath of allegiance (*bay'ah*). All their hopes lie in him who is one of them and reflects the spirit of the nation. In the Azharite view Nāṣir's revolution aims at the restoration of the early socialism of Islam.

IV

One may object to the preceding rather lengthy consideration of Azharite opinion of Egyptian policy. The Azhar was known to lend the support of its Islamic prestige and preeminence to Egyptian policy before 1952. Could not perhaps this extremist reinterpretation of Islam, especially its relation to socialism and a revolutionary Arab nationalism, reflect unavoidable obeisance to the power of an authoritarian regime that does not permit the proliferation of ideas or the free expression of opinions at variance with accepted policy? Or could it not also be the Azharite way of forestalling the development of Egyptian policy (socialism, Arabism, etc.) in a completely secular direction and orientation? Is al-Azhar, that is, eager to get the Egyptian ruling class to accept the premises that their revolution has better chances of success and that their Arab policy can be more convincing to other Arabs, if both are steeped in the values and virtues of Islam? For, in Egypt today, there are individuals and groups identified with the regime who would prefer a completely secular base for the revolution. These might be loosely characterized as the leftist writers, critics, economists, and journalists. They are products of the secular state school and university systems who, with the advent of the Free Officers Corps to power, have attained favored positions in their career and professional circles.

In the last two to three years the question of the role of religion in Egypt's revolution and policy has been brought into sharper focus by the appearance of a new debate among certain Egyptian writers. This debate centers its attention upon the meaning of the Arab-Islamic heritage. What is this heritage? If it is Islamic, must it also be Arab, and vice versa? Was this heritage one of intellectual weakness and stagnation regarding the ability of man to organize his life and carve out his destiny on earth, or was it a source of strength combining mind and work for continuous progress? Those Egyptians who take the latter position in this debate argue simply that man is the most important living being of the universe, as he is the strongest, by virtue of his intellect and perception. He uses his mind to devise organization and order for his existence and uses his hands to build his material environment and destiny. They further argue that the most important feature of human society is its evolution and constant change, two aspects of this society whose rate and character depend in the first place on man's physical and material environment. It appears that such a position sanctifies the human mind and capacity for physical work to support an existential secular conception of society. If this is the case, Egyptians holding this view are seriously challenging tradition and religion, for they are really claiming that man has the ability to discover the unknown as well as himself. They are also saying that these ideas should form the basis of modern education and culture if the Egyptian revolution aims to found a new and modern society.

What is interesting, though, about this position is that its advocates use Arabic-Islamic sources to advance it, namely, the writings of ibn-Khaldūn. They argue that ibn-Khaldūn's historical work had a definitely rational and sociological approach. If an Arab Muslim of the fourteenth century could attain that degree of sophistication, it is fatuous for modern Arabs and Muslims to languish in the quagmire of stifling tradition. On the contrary, this intellectual heritage constitutes the strongest tradition of rationality and, therefore, progress, which contemporary Arabs must adopt as a model for their programs of educational and cultural development.[53]

The adoption of reason as the basis for human endeavor is not, however, a novel idea or view in Egypt if one considers the works of Shiblī Shumayyil, Salāma Mūsā, Luṭfī al-Sayyid, or even those of Aḥmad Amīn and Tawfīq al-Ḥakīm. What is novel in the revived call for rationality today is the near-deification not only of the intellect but also of man's labor —especially manual labor—as is apparent in the writings of Muḥammad Sidqi.[54] Moreover, this new approach seeks to "socialize" the misfortune of the farming peasant, the *fallāh,* by bothering the conscience of the Egyptians, as both 'Abd al-Raḥmān al-Sharqāwī and Yūsuf Idrīs have tried to do in their writings.[55] The trials and tribulations of the hard-working, lowly public official and his family are projected into the daily awareness of the emancipated Egyptian and Arab nationalist in an effort to evoke his sympathy.[56]

Thus, even this secular debate to identify and assign a political and intellectual legacy for the revolutionary society is anxious to utilize profitably the Arab-Islamic connection. Al-Azhar and conservative Islamic groups may have no choice but to recognize the importance of an adapted and slanted Islam. Not only has the attack upon its earlier identification with rigid tradition lasted for almost seventy-five years, but it now emerges under the influence of ideas and ideologies that became widespread after World War II: socialism, Communism, and "development." Moreover, the government itself has ordered by decree the religious leaders and their institutions to join the bandwagon of modernization, so to speak. Thus, if a maverick shaykh, Khālid Muḥammad

Khālid, can call for a religion "in the service of the people," the Shaykh of al-Azhar himself can reconcile socialism with Islam.[57] If President Nāṣir can assert that Arabs are the only people who own a *qiblah* (direction for prayer), and that "the pilgrimage should have a potential political power," a Muslim nationalist associated with the revolutionary aims of Egyptian policy can popularize the central importance of the religion as a factor of Arab nationalism.[58]

V

So far we have tried to show the association and accommodation of Egypt's Arab policy with Islam and the measures taken by the Egyptian regime to mobilize the institutions and men of religion to explain this association in its various dimensions to the rest of the Arabs. Relevant to this explanation is the relationship of Islam to revolution and to socialism, to Arab nationalism and unity. The political establishment also decided that this explanation cannot be formulated effectively for both Egyptians and Arabs without the reform of religious institutions and, more significantly, without the reformulation of religious beliefs themselves in modern parlance which reflects the realities of power. I beg to submit that herein lies the possible contribution of Naṣīr's Egypt to the resolution of the as yet ambivalent attitude of the Arabs regarding the role and place of Islam in the evolution of a modern Arab society, nation, and state. If successful, Egypt may conceivably secure a measure of pre-eminence, if not hegemony, among radical Arab movements. To equate, however, this chance of success with ultimate Egyptian control of all Arab lands would, at this time, be a serious mistake.

The debate among Arabs regarding nationalism so far has raged among four major groups: (1) those who insist upon an Islamic base of solidarity and political action among all Arabs; (2) those who reject the Islamic base completely in favor of a secular formula of popular sovereignty; (3) those who wish to activate the Islamic base within the framework of modern policy orientations in such a way as to render it an efficacious mover to nationalist action throughout the Arab lands; and (4) those who do not consider this connection at all, but who react instinctively and emotionally as Muslims.

The third group appears of choice and necessity ascendant—even dominant—at the present time. The mistake of the older enthusiastic secularists who wished to reject the Islamic ethos is being avoided, and there seems to be popular recognition that strength is to be derived from the revival of one's own heritage. For even when we speak of language, culture, and history as factors in Arab nationalism, we find that for the Arabs all three of these elements have been closely connected with Islam. Under these circumstances, there seems to be a return to the idea of strengthening the Arab, but essentially Islamic, community. The return, however, does not represent a complete reversal in Egyptian thinking. Rather, it seeks to avoid the pitfalls of both apologia and fundamentalism and to concentrate instead on freeing Islam from the shackles of its own traditional inertia through reinterpretation. But reinterpretation is specifically a theological task, and what one perhaps confronts in Egypt is an attitude of accommodating Islamic ideas to the situation of the community. This attitude, I beg to submit further, is most interesting and pregnant with possibilities, for Islam could always be accommodated despite the argument that the gate of *ijtihād* has been closed for centuries: *ijtihād* pertains really to theological interpretation. The accommodation of Islam, however, to the practical situation of the community is particularly within the reach of forceful and successful rulers: *man ishtaddat waṭ'atuhu wajabat ṭā'atuhu* (It is a religious duty to obey those who are powerful). Ever since Muḥammad 'Abduh's first serious attempts to reform Islamic dogma, there has been a split in the ranks of the Egyptian *'ulamā'* regarding the reform of Islam and related problems of modernization. Although it is fair to say that the use of the *'ulamā'* for political purposes is a basically un-Islamic practice, their gradual bureaucratization by the Muḥammad 'Alī dynasty and state established a tradition in Egypt of the control of the men and institutions of religion by whatever regime is in power. Similarly, the control of *awqāf* (endowments) by the state deprived al-Azhar and its affiliated institutions of their financial independence, thus placing them also under state control.

It is difficult to assume that the Azharites are really evolving any systematic political or revolutionary ideology based on Islam. Their educational and other activities rather represent an attempt to accommodate Islam to the requirements of an authorized policy. It is therefore safer and more accurate to speak of Egyptian policy than of Egyptian ideology. The latter is hard to ascertain from the record of the military regime so far, according to the accepted criteria of ideological formulation. What the Azharites are therefore doing in the final analysis is nothing more or less than the bidding of the ruler.

In 1957 the present writer argued that "developments in the Arab countries tend to undermine the identification of national aspirations with a revived and active Islam." [59] By 1961–62, on the strength of evidence forthcoming from Egypt, the writer was forced to abandon this position and to argue instead that until patriotism as distinguished from nationalism [60] crystallizes among members of the Arab communities, a nationalist interpretation of Islam remains the most efficient formula of consensus.[61] If Islam can also be interpreted in such a way as to sanction the policies and ideas required to revolutionize and modernize Arab society, its instrumentalism in politics is augmented for the benefit of those who use it. But it is often dangerous to develop or extract political theories from religion. In addition to being the most perfect religious message of God to man after a succession of imperfect revelations, Islam is singularly distinguished from other religions as a sacred juridical system. Essentially, it does not prohibit theoretical speculation about the nature of society, politics, and human behavior. But, since Islam represents the most perfect revelation of God to man and the most satisfactory legal system for the regulation of the affairs of man and society, speculation about such matters is by definition limited to a process of deduction from given data and premises. Thus, the most advanced and systematic intellectual activity in Islam has consisted of compiling learned works on the sacred law. When the sacred law was discussed in relation to the state and the head of state—namely, the caliphate—it provided the basis for Muslim juridical thought and an interest in constitutional law. Any theoretical political speculation about the nature of the state and authority has been characterized by idealizations of political types.

Intellectual activities (even intellectual movements) in Islamic societies—particularly those that dealt with the state, power, and authority—have often, if not always, emanated from established authority (i.e., from the ruler). And this was particularly the situation in nineteenth-century Egypt. For a while, one might argue, the Western-influenced and Western-educated liberals, such as the late Aḥmad Luṭfī al-Sayyid and his colleagues at the turn of the century, essayed genuine speculation upon theoretical questions of politics, society, and man. But this kind of speculation and intellectual endeavor was completely outside the fundamental religious framework of Islam, and was short-lived. By 1930, enlightened liberal thought was discredited in Egypt and a variety of authoritarian mass movements and religious fundamentalist ideas came into fashion. With the rise to power of a military junta in 1952, free speculation upon basic issues of power and political organization was prohibited. Speculation and theoretical exercise once more emanate from established authority, or from the ruler. The latter, moreover, has decreed the casting of Egyptian policy in a dual but not mutually exclusive direction—a presumably modern socialist one, whose principles and inspiration derive from an outside, non-Islamic source, and a local traditional one, Islam. The fact that the ruler finds it necessary to do this, given his declared intentions of bringing about revolutionary change both in Egypt and the rest of the Arab lands, is an indication and admission of the significant and basic relationship between Islam and his policy abroad. It is in this relationship, I suggest, that one can take a long-range view of the use of Islam as an instrument in Egyptian foreign policy.

NOTES

1. See *The National Charter of the United Arab Republic,* May 21, 1962 (Cairo: U.A.R. Information Department, 1962).

2. See Albert Hourani, *Arabic Thought in the Liberal Age, 1798–1939* (London, 1962); Nadav Safran, *Egypt in Search of Political Community* (Cambridge, Mass., 1962); and Jamal M. Ahmed, *The Intellectual Origins of Egyptian Nationalism* (London, 1960). One of the main themes in the present writer's forthcoming volume, *A History of Modern Egypt, 1800–1960,* deals with this response.

3. Professor Vernon McKay deals with Islam in Africa in this volume.

4. *Collected Speeches of President Nasser,* January–March, 1960.

5. *Ibid.,* April–June, 1960.

6. *Ibid.*

7. *Ibid.*

8. *Ibid.,* October–December, 1960.

9. See Muḥammad Ibrāhīm Ḥamzah, *Ishtirakīyat al-islām wa al-ishtirakīyah al-gharbīyah* (Cairo, 1961), No. 12 in the series "Dirāsāt fī al-Islām," issued by the Higher Council for Islamic Affairs, Ministry of Endowments. In his tract, Ḥamzah refers (p. 7) to the Prophet Muḥammad as *"al-ishtirākī al-awwal"* ("the first socialist").

10. The term "religious institution" as used here does not mean the existence of an organized religious hierarchy or priesthood such as exists in Christianity,

but rather denotes the majority of religious leaders and teachers, as well as the religious and educational institutions and organizations, which are primarily concerned with teaching and maintaining the Islamic faith and tradition. An institution or organization similar to the Church does not exist in classical Islam.

11. See his "An Interpretation of Islamic History," *Journal of World History*, Vol. 1 (July, 1953), pp. 39–62.

12. See Aḥmad Ḥasan al-Zayyāt, editor of the *Journal of the Azhar,* in an editorial entitled "An Open Letter to the President," proclaiming the Fourth Golden Age of Islam under President Nāṣir, in *Majallat al-Azhar,* Vol. 34 (January, 1963), pp. 573–75. "The light of your judicious, balanced, and calm Charter will extend to every person and every land, as was extended the word of God, because it [the Charter] is the truth which God has placed in His *Sharī'ah* and the program (*manhaj*) which He devised for all His creatures." The other three Golden Ages in Islam, according to al-Zayyāt, were: the Age of al-Rashīd and his son al-Ma'mūn in Baghdad, the Age of al-'Azīz and his son al-Ḥākim in Cairo, and the Age of al-Nāṣir and his son al-Ḥakam in Cordova.

13. The writer has argued this point intensively in a forthcoming essay entitled "Islam and Revolution" from which the essay in this volume is adapted.

14. For example, the Cairo-versus-Mecca radio war as manifested in the psychological warfare and propaganda emanating from the Voice of the Arabs Radio in Cairo, on the one hand, and anti-Nāṣir broadcasts of Radio Mecca on the other.

15. Events in Europe during the 1920's and 1930's undoubtedly encouraged these trends and tendencies.

16. See his *Umm al-qura* (*The Mother of Cities*) (Aleppo, 1959). See also Muḥammad Aḥmad Khalafallāh, *al-Kawākibī, ḥayātuhu wa ārā'uhu* (Cairo, n.d.), and Sāmī al-Dahhān, *'Abd al-Raḥmān al-Kawākibī* (Cairo, n.d.). For an excellent discussion of al-Kawākibī's work, see Sylvia G. Haim, *Arab Nationalism: An Anthology* (Berkeley and Los Angeles, 1962), Introduction, esp. pp. 25–29.

17. Aḥmad Fū'ād al-Ahwānī teaches philosophy at Cairo University. In December, 1960, the Ministry of Culture published his tract, *al-Qawmīyah al-'arabīyah* (*Arab Nationalism*) (No. 27 in "al-Maktaba al-thaqafīyah" series of the Ministry), in which he discusses the role of religion in the genesis of an Arab national ideology. Dr. Muḥammad al-Bahī was Chancellor of al-Azhar University until September, 1961. Now Minister of Endowments, he continues to act as Chancellor of the University. Shaykh Shalṭūṭ, Imām and Rector of al-Azhar Mosque, publicly declared the Islamic sanction of Egypt's socialist laws of July, 1961, in a long pronouncement published in the official newspaper, *al-Goumhouriyya* (*al-Jumhurīyah*), December 22, 1961. (Shaykh Shalṭūṭ died in Cairo, June 16, 1964.)

18. See *Khutab al-ra'īs Jamāl 'Abd al-Nāṣir,* November, 1961–February, 1962, pp. 107 and 113.

19. See his *Modern Trends in Islam* (Chicago, 1947), pp. 106–29. The other two tendencies, according to Gibb, were for (1) a Pan-Islamic idea of a spiritual caliphate, and (2) a complete dissolution of the institution and its replacement by modern national sovereignty.

20. See Aḥmad Shafiq Pasha, *Ḥawlīyat Miṣr al-Siyāsīyah* (Cairo, 1925, 1929),

Vol. I, pp. 119–21; Vol. III, pp. 40–391. See also Elie Kedourie, "Egypt and the Caliphate 1915–1946," *Journal of the Royal Asiatic Society,* Parts 3 and 4, 1963, pp. 208–48.

21. See Shaykh 'Alī 'Abd al-Rāziq, *al-Islām wa uṣūl al-ḥukm* (Cairo, 1st and 2d eds., 1925); French translation by L. Bercher, "L'Islam et les bases du pouvoir," *Revue des études islamiques,* Vol. 7 (1933), pp. 353–91, and Vol. 8 (1934), pp. 163–222; and A. Sanhoury, *Le Califat* (Paris, 1926).

22. For a brief appraisal of the Islamic Congress, see the writer's *The Egyptian Army in Politics* (Bloomington, Ind., 1961), Ch. VII. In his *The Philosophy of the Revolution,* President Nāṣir projected the thought, "The Pilgrimage should have a potentially powerful significance." Writing elsewhere, Nāṣir asserted that the Arabs are the only people who own a *qiblah* (direction of prayer). See *al-Hilāl,* Vol. 65 (January, 1957), Special Issue, "Our Arab Nation."

23. For example, President Nāṣir's well-known introduction to his public rally speeches, "As is my practice and custom, I always try to keep you abreast of what is happening."

24. The writer used the term "Second Revolution" originally in his "Nasser's Second Revolution," *SAIS Review,* Vol. 6 (Spring, 1962), pp. 3–9.

25. Victory Day Speech, Port Said, U.A.R., *Arab Political Encyclopedia,* Documents and Notes, Tenth Year, December, 1961 (Cairo: Information Department), pp. 131–32.

26. See *Charter,* p. 94.

27. See the interesting biographical work of Dr. Fakhr al-Dīn al-Aḥmadī al-Ẓawāhirī, *al-Siyāsah wa al-Azhar* (*Politics and al-Azhar*) (Cairo, 1945), which is presumably based on the memoirs of Shaykh Muḥammad al-Aḥmadī al-Ẓawāhirī, Shaykh of al-Azhar, 1929–35. See also Shaykh 'Alī 'Abd al-Rāziq, *Min āthār Muṣṭafā 'Abd al-Rāziq* (Cairo, 1957). There are numerous works by Egyptians on the history of al-Azhar and the various attempts at reform. Bayard Dodge, *Al-Azhar, A Millenium of Muslim Learning* (Washington, D. C., 1961) lists the various reform measures and laws, but is not useful as an analytical treatise on al-Azhar and its problems. See also "Azhar," *Encyclopaedia of Islam* (new ed., 1960), Vol. I, pp. 813–21.

28. The text of the law, together with the Explanatory Memorandum of the Minister of State, are readily available in *Majallat al-Azhar,* Vol. 33 (July, 1961), pp. 237–64. A French translation of the Explanatory Memorandum is found in *MIDEO,* Vol. 6 (1959–61), pp. 474–84.

29. Writing in 1962, Ḥasan al-Ashmūnī stated that there were 3,022 Egyptian teachers abroad in twenty Afro-Asian countries in 1959–60, and that the number of foreign students studying in Egypt in the same year numbered 14,349. "Thus," he says, "the Arabs have retrieved their glories." See his tract, *Mujtama' unā al-jadīd wa al-Sharī'ah al-islamīyah* (*Our New Society and the Sharī'ah*), No. 23 (November 12, 1962) in the series "Dirāsāt fī al-Islām," of the Higher Council for Islamic Affairs, Ministry of Endowments (Cairo, 1962), p. 74. In February, 1959, al-Azhar published a 64–page brochure, *al-Azhar fī suṭūr,* aimed at non-Egyptian readers and audiences. It contains statistics about Azhar enrollments and offerings to foreign students.

30. The regime also has paid special attention to the efforts of the Department of Islamic Affairs and Studies of the Ministry of Endowments, which sponsors essay and book competitions among Muslim students in Egypt and

elsewhere. The Department's journal *Minbar al-Islām* (*The Pulpit of Islam*), founded in 1960, complements the *Journal of the Azhar* in many ways. It also publishes a series of popular monographs on Islamic subjects. (See *MIDEO*, Vol. 6 [1959–61], pp. 470–72.) An interesting series of lectures delivered at al-Azhar by leading Egyptian writers, teachers, and scholars, under the auspices of Shaykh Shalṭūṭ, the Rector, was published in Cairo in 1960. The theme of most of these lectures is the relationship between Islam and the requirements of a modern society.

31. Al-Ashmūni, *op. cit.*, p. 75.

32. Friday Sermon by Anwar al-Sadat in al-Azhar on March 22, 1959, reported in *al-Ahram*, March 23, 1959.

33. See Muḥammad al-Bahī, "al-Quwā al-sha'bīyah wa kaifah tu 'abba' naḥwah al-ishtirākīyah al-'arabīyah," *Majallat al-Azhar*, Vol. 33 (January, 1962), pp. 926–39.

34. See Aḥmad Ḥasan al-Zayyāt, "'Ām jadīd 'alā Azhar jadīd," *Majallat al-Azhar*, Vol. 34 (June, 1962), p. 3.

35. *Ibid.*, p. 2.

36. *Ibid.*

37. See his "al-Ishtirākīyah al-samāwīyah li al-ummah," *Majallat al-Azhar*, Vol. 34 (January, 1963), pp. 576–79.

38. See his editorial, "al-Īmān wa al-istiqāma ṭarīq al-amn wa al-salām," *op. cit.*, Vol. 34 (October, 1962), pp. 6–9.

39. See his editorial, "al-Shakṣīyah al-dīnīyah lijamā' at al-muslimīn," *op. cit.*, Vol. 33 (April, 1962), pp. 1291–95. Shalṭūṭ's approach to the Islamic community in this editorial is similar to President Nāṣir's interpretation of the significance of the pilgrimage and the *qiblah*.

40. See his editorial, "Mawqif al-islām min al-mustaghillīn," *op. cit.*, Vol. 33 (March, 1962), pp. 1168–75.

41. This view is more strongly expressed by Aḥmad Ḥasan al-Zayyāt. See his "al-Jazīrah al-'arabīyah tantafiḍu marratan ukhrā," *Majallat al-Azhar*, Vol. 34 (November, 1962), pp. 325–88, in which he discusses openly the situation in the Yemen and the "tyrannical" ruling houses of Jordan and Saudi Arabia.

42. See his English editorial, "The Message of al-Azhar After Its Reorganization," *Majallat al-Azhar*, Vol. 33 (January, 1962), pp. 16–20.

43. *Ibid.* In a speech at the ibn-Khaldūn festival, Shalṭūṭ laid greater stress on the Arabism of the religion when he said: "The Arab *ummah* was the nucleus of the elite leadership of the Islamic community when it carried Islam's message and spread it eastward and westward." See "Kalimāt al-imām al-akbar fī mahrajān ibn-Khaldūn," *op. cit.*, pp. 907–9.

44. See the interesting article by Maḥmūd Hoballah, "al-Islām wa al-'ālam," *Majallat al-Azhar*, Vol. 34 (January, 1963), pp. 593–600.

45. See his editorial, "Sayyidi al-ra'īs," *Majallat al-Azhar*, Vol. 34 (January, 1963), pp. 573–75.

46. See especially his *al-Fikr al-islāmī al-ḥadīth* (Cairo, 1957).

47. "An Idea and Its Utilization," *Majallat al-Azhar*, Vol. 34 (July, 1962), pp. 16–20.

48. "The Duty of al-Azhar Toward the Mobilization of the National Power," *op. cit.*, Vol. 33 (April, 1962), pp. 14–23.

49. *Ibid.* Al-Bahī argues further that the over-all objective of the revolution, the Charter, and the Reorganization Law of al-Azhar is to gear Islamic values

to the modern world. Thus, he ends his article: "Praise be to God for the advent of the revolution and its leaders." In his article, "al-Tadayyun durūraton li-ḥayāt al-ummah wa al-afrād," *Majallat al-Azhar,* Vol. 33 (March, 1962), pp. 1250–55, Muḥammad al-Nawāwī considers Nāṣir as the leader who is recapturing the true religious base of the nation.

50. Al-Bahī also argues that the leaders of the revolution which aims to mobilize national power toward socialism must be "naturally selected" (*op. cit.*). This is also the thesis of Ḥasan al-Ashmūni, *op. cit.,* namely, the reconciliation of the socialist laws of July, 1961, the program of the National Charter with Islam. Muḥammad Ḥamzah, on the other hand, considers the revolution as the force that will restore early Islamic socialism. See his *al-Ishtirakīyah al-islamīyah wa al-ishtirakīyah al-gharbīyah* (Cairo, 1961), "Dirāsāt fī al-Islām" Series of the Higher Council for Islamic Affairs, Ministry of Endowments, No. 12, pp. 99 ff. Al-Ashmūni, *op. cit.,* moreover, argues that Egypt's new socialist and revolutionary society is based on the *Sharī'ah;* that the socialist laws of July, 1961, were inspired by the heritage of Islamic values; in short, that the majority of legislative acts by the revolution since 1952 are consonant with the spirit of the sacred law—a link between the past and the present. As for al-Bahī's "naturally selected leaders" for the revolution, Ashmūni supports this view by arguing that the revolution and the new society are led by a head of state who through the *bay'ah* acquires the confidence and trust of the people. Conversely, the people place all their hopes in him, as he is one of them.

51. Al-Zayyāt claims that in April, 1940, he said in his journal *al-Risālah,* "O God we ask Thee for the shepherd who will turn away the wolf . . . who will reconcile faith with reason, and private with public interest and welfare. . . . All these attributes O our Lord will be found in one man, closest to the expected Mahdi and the promised Jesus." Nāṣir has presumably fulfilled this entreaty to the Heavens in 1940, so that all al-Zayyāt and Egyptians have to do now is repeat the formula, "We ask the Lord to prolong Your rule and strengthen Your power," i.e., the rule and power of President Nāṣir. As usual, there is no conception of a limited duration for the tenure of public office or power by one man.

52. Al-Zayyāt, *op. cit.,* Vol. 34 (January, 1963), pp. 573–75.

53. See, for example, the interesting book by Rushdi Ṣāliḥ, *Rajul fī al-Qāhirah* (Cairo, n.d.), and his article "Tārīkh ibn-Khaldūn yantamī li al-ḥaḍārah al-'arabīyah wa al-lughah al-'arabīyah," *al-Kitāb,* October, 1961, pp. 28–39.

54. See, for instance, his *al-Aidī al-khashīna* (Cairo, 1958).

55. See, for example, al-Sharqāwī, *al-Arḍ* (Cairo, 1954); an English translation, by Desmond Stewart, *Egyptian Earth,* appeared in London, 1962; and Yūsuf Idrīs, *Hādithat sharaf* (Beirut, 1958). Al-Sharqāwī has recently published an interesting book, *Muḥammad Rasul al-ḥurrīyah* (*Muḥammad, Apostle of Freedom*) (Cairo, 1962). See a critical review of this book in *Majallat al-Azhar,* Vol. 34 (June, 1962), pp. 106–9.

56. See the famous trilogy by Najib Mahfūz, *Bayn al-qaṣrayn, Qaṣr al-shawq,* and *al-Sukkarīyah* (Cairo, 1956–57). Generally on the intellectuals, see the writer's "al-Muthaqqaf al-'Arabī wa al-mujtma' al-ḥadīth" ("The Arab Intellectual and Modern Society"), *HIWAR,* Vol. 1 (May–June, 1963), pp. 41–51, and the response to it in the Cairo newspaper *al-Goumbouriyya,* June 13 and 19, 1963.

57. See Khālid Muḥammad Khālid, *al-Dīn fī khidmat al-sha'b* (Cairo, n.d.), and Shaykh Shaltūt in *al-Goumhouriyya,* December 22, 1961.

58. Aḥmad al-Ahwānī, *al-Qawmīyah al-'arabīyah* (Cairo, 1960).

59. "Recent Developments in Islam," *Tensions in the Middle East,* ed. P. W. Thayer (Baltimore, 1958), p. 178.

60. For an interesting distinction between these two concepts, see Bernard Lewis, *The Middle East and the West* (Bloomington, Ind., and London, 1964), Ch. 4.

61. See "Dilemmas of Political Leadership in the Arab Middle East," *American Political Science Review,* Vol. 55 (March, 1961), pp. 103–11; and "Foreign Policy of Egypt," *Foreign Policy in World Politics,* ed. Roy C. Macridis (2d ed.; Englewood Cliffs, N. J., 1962), pp. 335–59.

The Impact of Islam on Relations Among the New African States*

By Vernon McKay

Islam is part and parcel of the daily life of 90 million Africans, but it is difficult to isolate clear evidence of Islamic influences on foreign relations as opposed to domestic affairs. This is particularly true in Africa south of the Sahara. Moreover,

* The author is indebted to Jon Kraus for research assistance in the preparation of this paper. Mr. Kraus is a Ph.D. candidate in the Program of African Studies at the School of Advanced International Studies of The Johns Hopkins University.

even in Egypt, which provides the most conspicuous case of the use of Islam as an instrument of foreign policy, the task of separating Pan-Islamic influences from Pan-Arabism, Afro-Asianism, Egyptianism, Nasserism, and Pan-Africanism is almost insuperable.

In most African states, the shaping of foreign policy is in the hands of a few leaders, who are primarily concerned with domestic problems and have little experience and training in foreign affairs. They tend to react to foreign issues on a day-to-day basis and to make foreign policy statements that strengthen their positions at home but do not always reflect their personal convictions. The head of state often predominates in the making of foreign policy. Nine of Africa's presidents, two of its kings, and one of its prime ministers are Muslims. But Senegal, with an 80 per cent Muslim population has a Catholic president, and Chad, with more than 50 per cent Muslims, has a Protestant president. Several other states with significant Muslim minorities have Christian chief executives—Ethiopia with about 30 per cent Muslims, Sierra Leone with 25 per cent, and Ivory Coast, Liberia, Upper Volta, and Tanganyika, each with about 20 per cent.

However, the differing religions of chiefs of states are much less important than the central fact that most African leaders are highly secular in tone, tenor, and outlook. Many Muslim leaders have had Western educations and are as anxious as their Christian counterparts to modernize their countries. Some are more revolutionary than others, but all are attempting to overcome the obstacles to modernization; they find that tribal traditionalism and religious conservatism are among the chief barriers to the adaptation of Africa to life in the twentieth century. Most African leaders either attempt to deny the traditional chiefs and religious leaders any appreciable political power or, in states where reformist leaders are dependent for political power upon the support of conservative elements, they try to utilize these conservative forces as vehicles of modernization.

Before individual countries are examined as case studies of the impact of Islam on foreign relations, a brief sketch of the way Islam spread through Africa is essential. After sweeping westward through North Africa in the seventh century, it slowly spread southward across the Sahara along the trade routes of the old camel caravans. In the eleventh century the Almoravids, a militant group of Berber religious ascetics originating in what is now called Mauritania, pledged themselves to revive the original purity of the Muslim faith. Capturing the ancient kingdom of Ghana in 1076, they moved northward to win control of northwestern Africa all the way to Algiers, and then crossed the straits into Spain to defeat a Christian army at Zallarca in 1086. The era of greatest Islamic expansion, however, did not come until the nineteenth century—in the belt of savannah grasslands just south of the Sahara. In this "Broadway of Africa," to use a phrase of the geographer Ellen Semple, several militant leaders, including al-Ḥājj 'Umar in the western Sudan, 'Uthmān dan Fodio in Nigeria, and the Mahdī, Muḥammad Aḥmad, in the eastern Sudan, launched a number of successful *jihāds*. The resulting Muslim states were later taken over by the European colonial powers during the partition of Africa late in the nineteenth century. This European conquest enabled Christian missionaries to establish schools and make many converts in new tropical areas. But in those Sudanic regions where Islam was already established, British and French officials at times tended to adapt colonial administration to it, giving it favored treatment in Northern Nigeria and parts of French West Africa.[1]

Today, in addition to the 45 million Muslims in the five North African countries on the Mediterranean, there are perhaps another 45 million south of the Sahara. There are also 36 million Christians in the whole continent, including 17 million Roman Catholics, 13 million Protestants, 5 million Copts, and perhaps 1 million followers of African separatist churches and prophet movements. Nearly half of all Africans, however, still cling to their traditional animist religions. Christian missionaries in Northern Nigeria informed me in 1947 that the local rate of conversion was seventeen Muslims for one Christian, but recent guesses as to the over-all rate of conversion give the Muslims a three-to-one edge over the Christians.[2]

It is beyond the scope of this chapter to summarize the many explanations for the success of Islam in Africa south of the Sahara. It will suffice to cite one clear and simple reason given by an African Muslim, Amadou Hampaté Ba, formerly Director of the Institute of Scientific Research in Bamako and now Mali's Ambassador in the Ivory Coast:

> The process of passing from animism to Islam is made as easy as possible. The new convert is not bound by all the obligations, prayers, fasts and charities that are the duty of Moslems. We think that it would be too difficult to make this break all at once. We only ask him to make one promise: to send his children to the Koranic school. Then the children, educated in the religion of the Prophet, will fulfill all the obligations of the believers.[3]

It is especially relevant in a study of foreign relations to note another observation of Hampaté Ba. Islam, he believes, has adapted itself so well to the African Negro world that the faith has been profoundly affected. "The Negroes," he writes, "have cut a coat of their own measure out of Islam." In tropical Africa, Islam "takes on a much less combative and aggressive tone" than in North Africa or the Middle East. Other observers, including Sir Hamilton Gibb, have also been impressed by the calm depth of religious devotion among many West African Muslims in contrast to religious attitudes in certain other Islamic areas.

II

Let us accept the premise that Islam differs in Africa north and south of the Sahara. The two regions can then be examined separately in the search for those differences and similarities that might affect relations among states.

The percentage of Muslims in each African state is shown on the map on page 163. This chapter will deal with selected countries in which the number of Muslims has attained significant proportions—in North Africa, and in the Sudanic belt from Senegal to the Somali horn. The deliberate use of Islam as an instrument of foreign policy is most evident where 90 to 99 per cent of the population is Muslim—the five North African territories and Mauritania and Somalia. In the Sudanic territories that have a 50 to 80 per cent Muslim population, Islam influences domestic politics, but is less evident in international affairs. In this region Senegal, Guinea, Northern Nigeria, Cameroon, Chad, and the Sudan will be discussed. Below the Sudanic territories are states with Muslim minorities running from 5 per cent to 30 per cent. Ghana, Sierra Leone, Upper Volta, and Tanganyika will be briefly considered.

Let us first survey the states of mixed religious composition in Africa south of the Sahara. Many of the countries below the Sahara enshrine the principle of secularity in their constitutions, in contrast to those North African countries—Libya, Morocco, and Tunisia—whose constitutions proclaim Islam to be the religion of the state. For example, Article I of the Senegalese constitution and the preamble to the constitution of Chad proclaim the state "secular, democratic, and social." Article I in the constitution of Mali, Article I in that of Cameroon, and Article II in that of Upper Volta declare the state to be "democratic, secular, and social." In Guinea, Article 41 of the constitution asserts that "Freedom

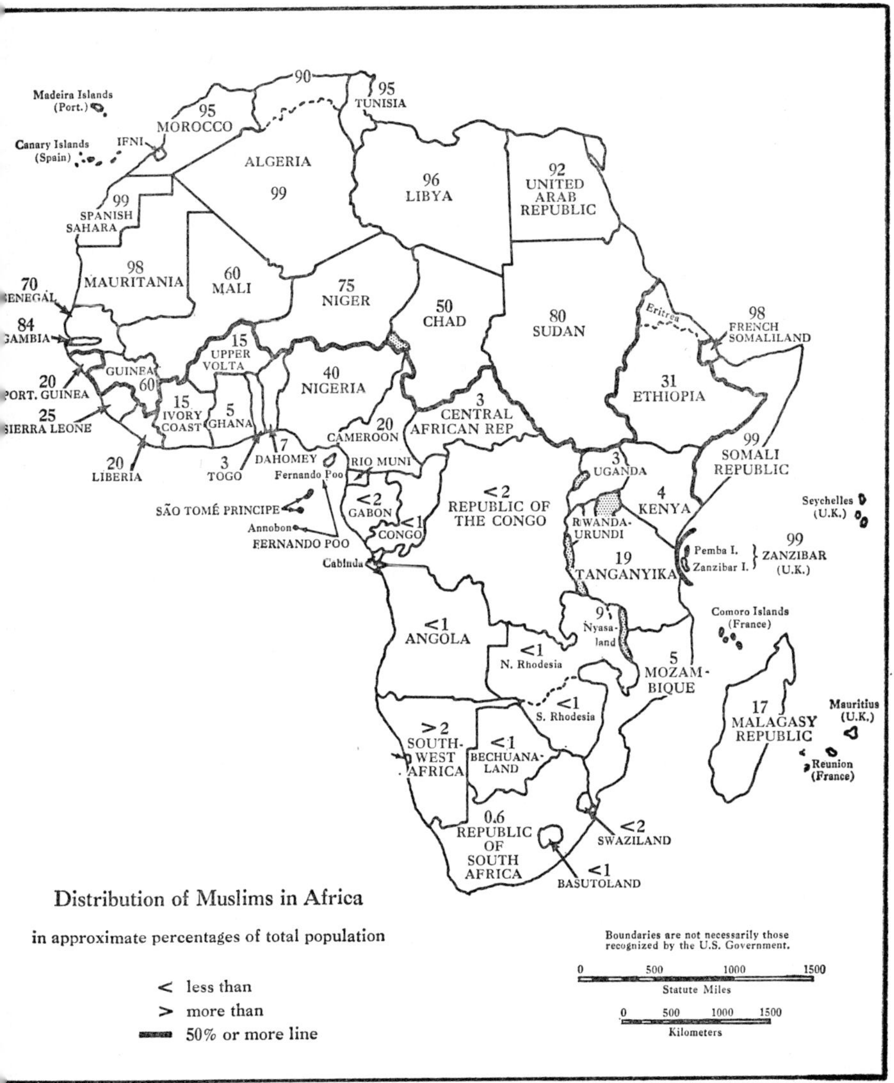

Distribution of Muslims in Africa

in approximate percentages of total population

ce: Adapted from the maps used in Jacques Baulin, *The Arab Role in Africa* (Baltimore, 1962), pp. 12-13.

of religion shall be assured to all citizens by the secularity of schools and state."

President Sékou Touré and 65 per cent of his countrymen are Muslims, but one finds little reference to Islam in the prolific writings and speeches of the President. In January, 1959, he announced that within two years all schools in Guinea would be nationalized. When he kept his word, he aroused strong protests, not from the Muslims, but from the Roman Catholics. His response was to expel the Catholic Archbishop and, with somewhat less than sociological accuracy, to declare: "A party is a social fact, a trade union is a social fact, a cooperative is a social fact. But a religion is not a social fact, it is an individual fact, or a spirit that is not engendered or modified by a social group, nor by the givens of time and space."[4] In his efforts to confine religion to the realm of the spiritual, Touré remarked in August, 1961, that all religions would be respected if they did not encroach on the political sphere. While government and party spokesmen have from time to time denounced as "fakes" some of the Muslim officials active in the villages, the government seeks to avoid public action to curtail traditional Muslim practices. In fact, it tends to identify itself with the Muslim majority where religious activity does not appear as a challenge to the authority of the government. For example, the construction of mosques is explicitly called for in Guinea's Three-Year Development Plan, and the first of 850 pilgrims to return from Mecca in 1961 were greeted formally and with much ado by governmental dignitaries of high rank.[5] Nonetheless, the domestic and foreign policies of Sékou Touré's government are basically secular and are little influenced by Islam. His anti-Zionist position at Casablanca in 1961 was primarily a political gesture of solidarity with the North African states in the Casablanca group.

In neighboring Senegal, which may be 80 per cent Muslim, we have already noted that President Léopold Sédar Senghor is a Catholic. His government is highly secular, but he still has to deal with Muslim religious leaders who remain, despite considerable sectarianism, the strongest traditional force in Senegalese politics. Senegal has more than one million Muslims split among three groups of the Tījānīyah sect and another 600,000 in the Muridīyah sect. The marabouts who lead these sects not only command religious respect but also hold strong positions in the Senegalese economy. They use their position to influence the votes of their followers, which brings them government subsidies and favors, particularly at election time.

The religious leaders were a major factor in bringing Senegal to vote *"oui"* rather than *"non"* on the 1958 de Gaulle referendum for autonomy within the Franco-African community. In November, they went on to form a Conseil Supérieur des Chefs Religieux du Sénégal, which sought to harmonize the country's political evolution with the precepts of Islam. The Conseil never became an effective political instrument, however, in large part because of internal rivalries and the dependence of the Muslim leaders on government subsidies. For the same reasons, the Parti de la Solidarité Sénégalaise (PSS), formed by the marabouts prior to the March, 1959, election, was also a failure. The conservatism of the marabouts was again evident in the position they took during the growing intraparty strife preceding Prime Minister Mamadou Dia's abortive *coup d'état* against President Senghor. Instead of backing their fellow-Muslim, Mamadou Dia, they supported their Christian President, in part because his views were more traditional than those of Dia.[6] Dia, incidentally, was sentenced to life imprisonment in May, 1963.

The weaknesses of the marabouts do not mean that they are powerless, but their influence is largely negative. In the words of William Foltz: "They can frequently block, hinder, or delay the application of governmental decisions which they feel directly menace their interests, but their divisions and lack of abilities in the modern political arena deny them any power of initiative."[7] The negative influence of the Senegalese marabouts seems characteristic of many traditional religious groups in Muslim Africa. Their ability to play a role in foreign relations, unless it be a negative role, is thus severely constricted.

On April 4, 1961, the first anniversary of Senegal's independence, President Senghor expressed the hope that the Afro-Malagasy Union (UAM) of French-speaking countries could bring about cooperation between "Negro-Africans and Arab-Berbers." He based this hope, however, not on the common bond of Islam, but on the common *Africanité* of the two groups.[8] And Senegal steers clear of the Arab-Israeli dispute, having carried on aid discussions with Israel since 1960. It is interesting to note, however, that although numerous governmental ministers from Senegal have visited Israel, as have nine heads of state in the UAM, neither Senghor nor Dia has made the trip. This suggests a cautious desire to avoid arousing any possible latent sympathy of the Senegalese Muslims for the Muslims of the Arab world. In this connection, it is worthy of note that the other UAM heads of state who have not visited Israel are Muslims—Daddah of Mauritania, which is 98 per cent Muslim, and Ahidjo of Cameroon and Diori of Niger, who govern peoples of differing religions.

Senegal's caution regarding the influence of Islam in relations among African states is also suggested by several remarks made in June, 1961, by Mamadou Dia on his return from a pilgrimage to Mecca. In response to a question on the possibility of an eventual union of Muslim states, Dia replied that "closer relations might be desirable among the Moslem states but they should be accompanied by certain guarantees so that no state under the pretext of Islamic unity could aim at intervention in the political life of other Moslem states."

In Dakar shortly afterward, he stated that he favored the convocation of a universal Muslim congress to enable Africans and Arabs to know one another better, provided, he warned, that the spiritual aspects of such a congress were not distorted and that it shied away from conflicts with other religions.[9]

Let us now examine the four countries that provide the best examples of states with the common problem of having Sudanic Muslims in the north and more Negroid peoples of animist or Christian faith in the south—Nigeria, Cameroon, Chad, and Sudan.

In Nigeria, Islam influences politics at the local and regional level, but very little in national and international affairs. The establishment of the Fulani emirates during the *jihād* of 'Uthmān dan Fodio early in the nineteenth century prepared the way for Islamic expansion through Northern Nigeria, and later through parts of the Western Region. The Muslim "establishment" in the North wields Islam as a powerful political instrument on the domestic scene. In the Federal Government, the Northern People's Congress is the leading party in the coalition government, but its leaders, notably the Prime Minister, Sir Abubakar Tafawa Balewa, are more sophisticated and undoubtedly more secular in outlook than many local leaders in the Northern Region itself. Aware of Nigeria's size and potential leadership role among the new African states, the Prime Minister has been loath to permit the Islamic inclinations of the North to influence Nigeria's attitude in inter-African or international affairs. Aside from the fact that the partner party in the coalition government, the National Council of Nigerian Citizens, would not allow Nigeria to convey the image of an Islamic state, Sir Abubakar realizes that good relations within the community of African states require a broad basis of mutual interests rather than the parochialism of a particular religious faith.

Many Nigerian politicians look askance at Nāṣir's Egypt.

In the North itself, the reformist Northern Elements Progressive Union viewed suspiciously the early "Pakistanization" tendencies of the rival Northern People's Congress, especially after the latter was visited by a delegation from Egypt. In mid-1962, the Premier of the Northern Region, Sir Ahmadu Bello, who heads the Northern People's Congress, aroused considerable protest by declaring himself in favor of a grouping of Islamic states. In his 1962 autobiography, however, Sir Ahmadu avoids expressing any Pan-Islamic opinions.[10] The Northern Region did protest against Nigerian technical assistance agreements with Israel, an action that aroused sharp criticism in the South. At one point the influence of Islam also led the Northern Government to hire a number of Muslim doctors from Pakistan. The Northerners were reportedly disillusioned with the experiment, however, when a majority of the Pakistani doctors proved unsatisfactory in the Nigerian environment.

Obafemi Awolowo, formerly Premier of the Western Region of Nigeria and erstwhile leader of the Action Group opposition in the Federal Parliament, has expressed deep antagonism toward Egypt:

> It is true that, physically and geographically, Egypt is in Africa. But apart from the fact that her entire political heart is in the Arab world, she has never regarded herself as having any social and cultural affinity with the black races of Africa. The United Arab Republic, the pet creature of Nasser, which has one foot in Africa and another in the Middle East, is the very antithesis of a workable African community. With his undisguised totalitarianism, and his territorial ambitions in Africa and the Moslem world, effective cooperation with Nasser, in any field at all, would be possible only if the black races of Africa were prepared to remain as satellites in Egypt's orbit.[11]

These hostile reactions from Nigeria have apparently influenced Egypt to modify its tactics in Africa. Cairo's recently inaugurated broadcasts in Hausa to Nigeria are from all accounts relatively free of appeals to Islamic solidarity, and even of the bellicose variety of anticolonialism sometimes heard in Voice of Africa programs from Egypt.

In the neighboring Republic of Cameroon, Islamic influences were involved in a bitter quarrel with Nigeria in the United Nations in 1960–61. The roots of President Ahmadou Ahidjo's governing party, the Union Camerounaise, are in the more conservative Muslim north. When the United Nations supervised plebiscites in the northern and southern sections of the trust territory of British Cameroons in 1960 and 1961, a curious split occurred. Sixty per cent of the Muslim northerners voted to join independent Nigeria, in contrast to 70 per cent of the southerners, who voted to join the independent Republic of Cameroon, formerly a French-administered trust territory. This result was politically adverse to Ahidjo because it denied him the support of fellow-Muslims from the northern British Cameroons, while adding potential opponents among the Christians and animists in the coastal area.

Ahidjo protested against "undemocratic irregularities" in the northern referendum. When the dispute came before the U.N. General Assembly, Cameroon accused Britain of permitting Nigerians to interfere with the voting. Before the debate began, Cameroon's Foreign Minister Okala declared that if his country did not get the support of the United States against Britain and Nigeria, he would "seek justice in the East." [12] When the General Assembly's Fourth Committee rejected their appeal, Cameroon's delegates angrily walked out, followed by the French and Belgian delegations and the representatives of a number of French-speaking African states.

If Ahidjo had continued to feel seriously threatened by this influx of non-Muslim voters, he might have carried the issue further, thus inciting a contentious irredentist movement. As it turned out, at least thus far, he has been able to govern a relatively stable and cohesive state, suppressing a rebellion in the Bamiléké area and developing the institutions of a federal structure to unite the southern part of the former British trust territory with his state. Once again, however, the paramountcy of politics over religion is evident. Ahidjo's primary interest in those northern Cameroonians who joined Nigeria was an interest in their votes, not in their fate as fellow-Muslims.

Northeast of Cameroon lies the most isolated of the former French territories, the Republic of Chad, which borders the northern and Muslim part of the Republic of Sudan for 600 miles. The cleavage between the Muslim north and the Christian-animist south is often divisive of national unity in Chad, which is about 50 per cent Muslim. The underdeveloped north seems willing to perpetuate tribal traditionalism and Muslim religious conservatism. Although the northern leaders are frequently divided, five of their political groups formed the Parti National Africain in 1962 to maintain the "Muslim tradition" in education and social matters and to strengthen Chad's relations with neighboring Muslim countries as ties with France are lessened.[13] However, the governing party, under President François Tombalbaye, a Christian, is the Parti Progressiste Tchadien, which has its strength in the Christian-animist south. It opposes tribalism, urges secularization of education and social life, and vigorously opposes any unification with neighboring Muslim states. In March, 1963, this friction between the two regions precipitated the dissolution of the National Assembly and the arrest of five leaders who were accused of "endangering the state's internal and external security by fomenting and supporting subversive activities." President Tombalbaye accused them of wanting to incite the Arab north against the African south by stirring up local and religious quarrels.[14]

The cleavage between an Arab-Muslim north and a

Negroid-animist south is even sharper in the Republic of Sudan, Africa's largest country. The President, General Ibrāhīm 'Abbūd, seeks to build national unity among his diverse peoples by developing a common educational system. In 1957 the Christian schools were nationalized. Many Christian missionaries, some of whom are suspected of contributing to the disaffection that led to a mutiny in 1955, are being expelled from the south. A considerable number of dissident Sudanese tribesmen who object to the tactics of the northerners fled across the border in 1962 to live with fellow-tribesmen in the Congo, Ethiopia, Kenya, and Uganda. To counter a movement for self-government for the 3 million Negroid people of the southern Sudan, General 'Abbūd dispatched an armed force of 6,000 troops to the southern border in October, 1962. Whatever his aims, General 'Abbūd's tactics have aroused sharp criticism. The Nigerian radio, in a broadcast to the rest of Africa on June 12, 1963, accused the Sudanese Prime Minister of "an accelerated plan to bully the south into accepting a thoroughly centralized system with a single educational program, a single language—Arabic, a single religion, and a single Islamic way of life."

Several years ago, before the November, 1958, military coup that brought General 'Abbūd to power, Sudanese politics was strikingly sectarian. Each of the two major parties was allied with a different Islamic religious group—the National Union Party with the Khatmīyah confraternity, and the Ummah Party with the Ansar Association, whose members venerated Sayyid 'Abd al-Raḥman al-Mahdī as the posthumous son of the Mahdī. The National Union Party and the Khatmīyah originally favored union with Egypt, while Ummah and Ansar championed Sudanese independence. After winning a 1953 election, however, the National Union Party leader, al-Azhari, turned away from the idea of union with Egypt and led the Sudan to independence on January 1, 1956.

The power of the secular trend in African politics soon began to strain the relations between the Islamic sects and the government. When al-Azhari sought to remove Sudanese politics from religious influences, the Ansar and Khatmīyah leaders, Sayyid al-Mahdī and Sayyid al-Mirghānī, joined hands against him in 1956. The Khatmīyah of al-Mirghānī broke away from the National Union Party, launched a new People's Democratic Party, and formed a coalition government with the Ummah to restore political leadership to men of religion. In Thomas Hodgkin's words, "It is almost as though Britain had a government which was publicly supported by the Archbishop of Canterbury, the Apostolic Delegate, and the Chief Moderator of the Church of Scotland." [15] This coalition government was pro-Western and hostile to those Sudanese who leaned toward nonalignment and identification with Arab nationalism.

By November, 1958, however, the Sudan was in economic, as well as political, trouble. Communists had gained a strong position in the trade unions. The allocation of the Nile waters was still in dispute with Egypt. In this crisis, al-Mahdī and al-Mirghānī appear to have reached another understanding, this time to support a coup by a military triumvirate headed by General 'Abbūd.

The conflict between secularization and Islamic sectarianism in Sudanese politics was thus outwardly suspended. In fact, however, General 'Abbūd's policies reflected a secularized, essentially nonreligious point of view. Once again, Islam, especially a contentious Islam, proved inadequate for political leadership.

III

From these six examples of sub-Saharan states with large Muslim populations—Guinea, Senegal, Nigeria, Cameroon, Chad, and Sudan—let us turn briefly to certain states in which Muslims are relatively small minorities—Ghana, Sierra Leone, Upper Volta, and Tanganyika.

Ghana has the lowest percentage of Muslims among these four, although estimates vary from 3.5 to 14 per cent of the Ghanaian population. Whatever the total, however, Ghanaian politics is highly secular, and President Kwame Nkrumah is well known for his insistence on keeping religion out of politics. A Muslim Association, founded in 1932, backed the candidates of Nkrumah's Convention People's Party in the 1951 elections. By 1954, however, the Muslim Association had turned against Nkrumah. It formed its own party and backed either its own candidates or, in constituencies where it had no candidates, it supported other anti-Nkrumah office-seekers. The reaction of the Nkrumah government, when Ghana became independent, was to put through an Avoidance of Discrimination Act in 1957 which banned political parties representing only special religious or ethnic communities. The Muslim Association Party then went into the opposition United Party.

At the international level, President Nkrumah's dislike of President Nāṣir's use of Pan-Islamic and Pan-Arab influences to further Egypt's interests abroad is well known. Although Ghana joined in a denunciation of Israeli neocolonialism at Casablanca in 1961, it has readily continued to accept Israeli investment and technical assistance. Nkrumah's wife is an Egyptian, but a Coptic Christian, not a Muslim. Ghana's reaction to Nāṣir's foreign policy was again revealed when it insisted on the closing of the United Arab Republic's cultural office in Accra in November, 1962.

Estimates of the percentage of Muslims in Sierra Leone vary from 16 to 25 per cent of the total population. The leader of the opposition party is a Muslim, but the primary division in Sierra Leone is ethnic, not religious—a division between the Creole peoples of the coast and the tribes of the hinterland. At the Addis Ababa conference of the proposed

Inter-African and Malagasy Organization in May, 1963, Sierra Leone's Foreign Minister, John Karefa-Smart, had a tart exchange with the Foreign Minister of the United Arab Republic, Maḥmūd Fawzī. Karefa-Smart remarked that President Nāṣir "should let us know whether he belongs to Africa or not, and the meaning of his dream for an African Empire." Fawzī responded by accusing Sierra Leone of raising "irrelevant issues." [16]

In Upper Volta, which is 20 per cent Muslim, President Maurice Yaméogo is a Catholic, while the Paramount Chief of the largest ethnic group, the Moro Naba of the Mossi, is a recent convert to Islam. One wonders whether the Moro Naba's conversion may end the long history of Mossi resistance to Islam. Meanwhile, it might be facetiously argued, the case of Upper Volta suggests that Christianity has a more powerful impact than Islam on African foreign relations. At least President Yaméogo in 1962 told his people that when he visited Rome in 1960, he asked the Pope what he thought about Upper Volta's intention to work for its independence. The Pope replied: "My son, that is natural, take your independence, take it completely, but keep your friendship with France." During Yaméogo's 1962 reception at the Vatican, he received the papal blessing "that we in Upper Volta, Catholics, Muslims, Protestants, Animists, could continue in the right direction that we have started here." [17]

Along the east coast of Africa, Islam was brought in from the sea by Arabs and, in later years, by Muslims from India. South of Somalia, which is entirely Muslim, Islamic penetration is limited mostly to the coastal areas as far south as northern Mozambique. The Arab traders once had a monopoly of the slave trade through the Swahili coast into the Congo, and the memory of it still persists in Africa as a factor limiting Arab expansion. The Swahili people are Muslim Bantu coastal peoples with a considerable admixture of Arab stock. The word "Swahili" is said to be derived from an

Arabic word meaning "the coast people." The Swahili language has become a *lingua franca* for all of Tanganyika and certain neighboring areas as well. About 20 per cent of the 9.5 million people of Tanganyika are Muslim, and an All Muslim National Union exists but has made little headway as a political force. President Julius Nyerere is a Roman Catholic who is quite secular in politics and an advocate of racial harmony and moderation.

IV

Islam is naturally more influential in the foreign relations of the seven African states with populations from 90 to 99 per cent Muslim. These are Somalia and Mauritania, and the five Mediterranean countries—Morocco, Algeria, Tunisia, Libya, and the United Arab Republic.

Somalia is unique in tropical Africa for its homogeneity, despite a good deal of controversy among its clans. A country of more than 2 million inhabitants, it is not only 99 per cent Muslim, but most of its people are of common ethnic origin and speak dialects of a common Somali language. Outside Somalia, there are perhaps 30,000 Somalis in French Somaliland, 500,000 or more in the Ogaden Province of Ethiopia, and somewhere between 50,000 and 125,000 in the Northern Frontier District of Kenya. Somali nationalists have become avid irredentists. In their demands for unification of all Somalis, however, they include their Islamic faith as only one of their reasons, along with their common history, language, culture, "race," and "way of life."

Britain agreed to the unification of former British Somaliland with Somalia. In Kenya, however, it decided to create a seventh region for Kenya Somalis, a step that caused Somalia to sever diplomatic relations with the United Kingdom almost immediately. The French want to hold on to French Somaliland, and Ethiopia, which has a population perhaps

30 per cent Muslim, is one of the most vigorous of all opponents of the Pan-Somali movement. Ethiopia tries not to antagonize its Muslim neighbors. Despite its legendary dynastic ties with ancient Israel, and its technical assistance from Israel today, Ethiopia did not exchange consular representatives with Israel until 1956 and received its first Israeli ambassador only in 1962.

Somalis won support for unification at the 1957 Afro-Asian People's Solidarity Conference and the 1958 All-African People's Conference, but their efforts were unsuccessful amidst the cautious bipartisanship of the 1961 conference of African states at Monrovia. Ethiopia and Somalia are members of both the Monrovia group and the Pan-African Freedom Movement for East, Central, and South Africa. If the Somalis continue to press their claims, the resulting tension could have quite a disruptive effect on international relations. But how could one determine the extent to which Islam, as opposed to ethnic and other factors, would be responsible?

A second African irredentist movement in which Islam is involved is the adamant Moroccan demand to integrate Mauritania with Morocco. Morocco is a modified theocracy in which the head of state, King Ḥasan II, is also the spiritual leader. The irredentist claim has a religious character because it is based on the history of the Almoravids, the militant ascetics who swept northward through Morocco in the eleventh century. Part of the Moroccan case, as elaborated in its *Livre blanc sur la Mauritanie,* rests on the historical fact that for centuries the Muslims of this area have prayed in the name of the sultan of Morocco. The chief protagonist of Moroccan demands is 'Alāl al-Fāsī, Islamic scholar and leader of the Istiqlal Party, who was until early 1963 a government minister in charge of Islamic affairs.

Eighty per cent of the people of the Islamic Republic of Mauritania are of mixed Arab and Berber origin, while the remaining 20 per cent are Negroid peoples in the south. In a French-supervised referendum in September, 1960, the Mauritanians chose independence within the French Community. Since that date, President Mokhtar Ould Daddah has consolidated his regime, neutralized the opposition, and taken Mauritania into the United Nations.[18] As a result, Morocco has little or no chance of absorbing Mauritania. Nonetheless, the intensity of Moroccan demands increased in 1961 and early 1962.

Morocco's claims to Mauritania and other Saharan lands have aroused many antagonisms. Partly to recruit support for these claims, Morocco invited the other states now comprising the Casablanca group to meet in January, 1961. When these states decided to support Morocco, they antagonized the French-speaking states of the Afro-Malagasy Union. Good relations between Morocco and Tunisia were also jeopardized when Tunisia not only refused to support Morocco's claim but sent emissaries to Mauritania's independence celebration and sponsored its admission to the United Nations. Morocco's claims in Algeria's Saharan territory precipitated clashes in mid-1962 between Moroccan and Algerian forces in the Tindouf region. The Mauritanian issue also imperiled relations between France and Morocco. It has proved to be a serious obstacle in Pan-African political movements and inter-African economic cooperation.

Why was Moroccan behavior so quixotic? And how much was Islam to blame? In an interesting analysis of the irredentist appeal, Douglas Ashford concludes that it was primarily another case of using foreign policy to divert attention from domestic troubles. Islam no doubt provided part of al-Fāsī's motivation, but his irredentist agitation was largely disregarded by both the King and the young reformers for nearly two years after Moroccan independence. They were interested in the modernization of Morocco, not in foreign ventures, and they were embarrassed by al-Fāsī's behavior.

Why, then, did they change their minds and take up the irredentist banner in 1958? It was not because of Islam. It was the result of a variety of internal troubles that threatened to destroy nationalist solidarity. Threatened by the rise of a militant left-wing faction in 1958, the throne joined the Istiqlal irredentist campaign, a step which proved to be a useful patriotic device to revive the spirit of national unity. Ashford suggests that "the irredentist campaign may actually have had a desirable effect insofar as it brought Moroccans together during a period of internal strains and foreign disappointments." [19] It should be noted, however, that other "internal strains" appeared in 1963 when King Ḥasan sought to call a halt to Morocco's irredentist campaign. The King accepted the resignation of al-Fāsī, a sign that the *de facto* coalition between the throne and Istiqlal was coming to an end. Nonetheless, the King stayed away from the African "summit" meeting at Addis Ababa in May, 1963, and Morocco withdrew its representation because of the presence of a Mauritanian delegation.

The republican regimes in Algeria and Tunisia are more secular than Morocco's constitutional theocracy. It is true that in all three of these Maghribian countries Islam was used in various ways during the colonial era to strengthen the struggle for independence. In Algeria, Shaykh 'Abd al-Hamīd bin-Badis, who founded the Association of Reformist *'Ulamā'* in 1931, called for a return to the original purity and vigor of Islam as a means to independence. This movement was too religious in character, however, to come to terms with either emerging middle-class leaders such as Ferhat Abbas or the more proletarian types of the later National Liberation Front (FLN). Nonetheless, the FLN found Islam useful for its purposes too. In the words of the FLN newspaper, *al-Moujahid* (*The Struggler*):

> The spirit of Algerian Nationalism has been formed in the mould of Islamic culture and the Arabic language. Algeria, like Tunisia and Morocco, has been able to demonstrate the scope of its creative spirit in contributing to the realization and the progress of the Moslem civilization, of which it is one of the genuine depositories. . . . Like most Moslem nations it was during the centuries when Moslem civilization had reached its zenith that Algeria wrote the most beautiful pages of its history.[20]

Basically, however, the emergence of radical political leadership in Algeria confines the influence of Islamic religious leaders to the spiritual plane. Radicalism in Algeria may cause future trouble with Morocco. The rather sudden announcement of a Moroccan constitution in early November, 1962, was apparently stimulated in part by the rise of Ahmed Ben Bella (bin-Ballā) as Premier of Algeria. When Ben Bella was first released from incarceration in France, he promised Nāṣir 100,000 Algerians to drive Israeli Zionists into the sea, and early in 1963 rumors circulated that Algeria might join the United Arab Republic. Such rumors were soon quashed, however, when Mohammed Khider (Muḥammad Khidr), the Pan-Arab–oriented Secretary-General of the FLN, was dismissed.

The latest rumor is that Ben Bella "frankly aims," after consolidating his domestic power, to overthrow King Ḥasan in Morocco and President Bourguiba (Bū-Raqībah) in Tunisia. He might then become the head of the long-proposed Maghribian Confederation! It has also been suggested that Algeria, with French and American aid, is economically better off than Egypt, despite seven years of Algerian civil strife, and could become the leading nation in the Arab world. Immediately after Nāṣir's departure from a visit to Algiers in May, 1963, Ben Bella announced that French President Charles de Gaulle has been invited to visit him in the fall of 1963.[21] Many Algerians are said to believe that their country could have a greater future as a bridge between Europe and Africa than as a part of Nāṣir's Arab world. Ben Bella has also been cultivating leaders in Africa south of the Sahara. On May 24, 1963, he told the heads of African states assembled at the Addis Ababa conference that 10,000 Algerian volunteers were ready to fight in Angola.

In Tunisia, the leading Islamic reformer of the 1930's was the Old Destourian, 'Abd al-'Azīz Ta'albi. As in the case of bin-Badis in Algeria, however, his ideas could not compete successfully with the secular approach of the modernizers—in this case, the Neo-Destour leader Habib Bourguiba. Although Article I of the constitution of Tunisia proclaims that "Islam is its religion," Bourguiba abolished the monarchy of Sidi Lamine Bey, who was also the nominal religious head of Tunisia, on July 25, 1957.

Bourguiba is more of a reformer than a revolutionary, using persuasion rather than force, as indicated by the tentative character of his move toward ending the Muslim custom of fasting during Ramaḍān. He rejects the approach of those modernists who regard Islam as an obstacle to progress, but contends that "the sacred or revealed character of certain rules should not stand in the way of bold thinkers who question whether these rules are an asset to the progress of the Moslem people." In Bourguiba's view, if a reform is "in conformity with the well-understood interest of the community . . . one can surely find in the Sacred Texts a confirmation of one's opinion." [22] He is thus aware of the possibility of using Islam as an instrument to promote modernization and national solidarity. He is cautious about its usefulness as an instrument of foreign policy, however, rejecting Morocco's claim to Mauritania and Egypt's Pan-Islamic inclinations. Although Tunisia joined the Arab League in 1958, Bourguiba's poor relations with Nāṣir continued for some time, revealing the limitations of both Islamic and Arab solidarity.

In Libya, King Idrīs al-Sanūsī I is not only a constitutional monarch with considerable power, but is also the head of the Sanūsī sect to which most of the Cyrenaicans and some of the eastern Tripolitanians belong. In this federal regime, the Government is responsible to the King rather than to the Federal Assembly. The traditionalist character of the Libyan Government runs counter to the modernist regimes of neighboring Tunisia and Egypt, and might lead to bad relations in the future. Before political parties were banished, the major Tripolitanian party was inclined toward the United Arab Republic.

Majid Khadduri has described two major Libyan schools of thought regarding foreign policy. These are the "idealistic" school, which favors Arab unity on a socialist basis along with nonalignment in the Cold War, and the "Libyan or realistic" school, which has the support of King Idrīs and is now dominant. It favors good relations with the West and a "good neighbor" policy with all Arab countries. This policy includes membership in the Arab League, a neutral course with regard to disputes among other Arab countries, and the offer of Libyan services to reconcile Arab differences.[23]

The United Arab Republic, as already noted, uses Islam as an instrument of foreign policy more than any other African state. Like Bourguiba, President Jamāl 'Abd al-Nāṣir maintains that "the essence of religious messages does not conflict with the facts of our life." Conflict arises only when reactionaries exploit religion in order to impede progress. From this basic outlook the U.A.R.'s President has proceeded to develop his own way of using Islam to achieve his purposes. In domestic affairs he tries to induce the religious leaders to advocate modernization, and in foreign relations he uses the radio, the press, the universities, and other media to enhance Egypt's role in world affairs by developing Cairo as a center for spreading the message of Islam.

Egypt has had a long-standing interest in the North African coast and the Nile Valley, and students from Africa south of the Sahara have made their way to al-Azhar since at least the fifteenth century. Egypt's interest in Africa south of the Sudan did not become politically significant, however, until less than a decade ago. Africa is described as being in the "second circle" of Egyptian interests by Nāṣir in his 1953 book, *Egypt's Liberation: The Philosophy of the Revolution.* In a somewhat romantic vein Nāṣir wrote that "the peoples of Africa will continue to look to us, who guard their northern gate, and who constitute their link with the outside world." Nāṣir's paternalistic tone suggested from the beginning that Egypt would have trouble in learning how to deal with educated Negro Africans. "We will never in any circumstances," he wrote, "be able to relinquish our responsibility to support, with all our might, the spread of enlightenment and civilization to the remotest depths of the jungle." [24]

In August, 1956, an Egyptian program for Africa was outlined in the *Egyptian Economic and Political Review,* calling for increased diplomatic representation, radio broadcasts in African languages, establishment of religious and economic missions, scholarships for promising African students, an African Congress to meet annually in Cairo, and an Institute for African Affairs to study the "imperialist methods" of the colonial powers. The U.A.R. has undertaken numerous steps toward the fulfillment of this ambitious program. Cairo's radio transmitters now have several services to Africa: The Voice of Africa, seventy-three and a half hours a week in eight African languages, plus Arabic, English, and French; the Egyptian International Service, ten and a half hours a week to North Africa in Arabic and English; the Voice of the Arabs, thirty-four and a half hours per week to the Sudan in colloquial Arabic and seven hours to the Maghrib; and the Voice of Islam, a three-hour-a-week program conducted by al-Azhar.[25]

In the academic year 1962–63, al-Azhar had 1,666 African students from twenty-six different African countries, though apparently none from Islamic Northern Nigeria.[26] The United Arab Republic tries to develop a friendly atmosphere for these students in order to win their support for Egyptian values and aims. In 1960, the U.A.R.'s drama censor sent instructions to local film producers and directors to avoid giving the role of servants only to Negroes, which led the Egyptian review, *Nahdahtu Ifriqqīyah,* to comment in November: "The age of African servants is over. Now begins that of the Africans as thinking individuals." [27] Many students are given scholarships and all foreign students are housed together in the "City of Islamic Missions," a new center with forty residential buildings a mile and a half north of al-Azhar.[28] A recent report from Cairo, however, indicates that African students still encounter occasional discrimination there, just as they do in the United States, the Soviet bloc, India, and elsewhere.[29]

Whether by accident or design there is considerable confusion between Pan-Arab and Pan-Islamic propaganda in Egypt. In 1959 the Arab League, in issue No. 101 of *The Arab World,* published a map showing parts of Eritrea and French Somaliland as well as all of Chad, Senegal, Mali, Mauritania, and part of Niger as Arab! [30] At the same time, President Nāṣir has made it clear that he opposes the idea of a federation of Islamic states, which would conflict with the objectives of Arab nationalism. When the Africa Institute was outlined in 1956, the plan nonetheless linked religion and politics: "A section of this Institute is to be allocated for special studies by those who will be sent on missions from the Azhar and the Ministry of Education and Instruction. They will go to Africa for teaching, preaching, and giving lessons in the fundamentals of religion, so that they may by this means be able to preach Egyptian politics there." [31] Such linking of the Islamic religion with Arab politics often backfires by irritating the leaders of Africa. In both Libya and Somalia, Egyptian teachers have been accused of propaganda and undue interference in local affairs. On June 12, 1956, Somali petitioners complained to the United Nations Trusteeship Council that Egyptian teachers were threatening students that they would be divorced from Islam until Somalia cemented ties with Egypt. It was alleged that Egyptian propagandists were pressuring Somalia to join the Arab League when it became independent.

The export of Egyptian teachers is made possible by the prodigious output of Egypt's six universities, which have a total student body of well over 100,000. It is interesting to note that this fact was brought to the attention of the UNESCO Conference on Higher Education held in Tananarive, September 3–12, 1962. In view of its large university enrollment, the United Arab Republic, which already supplies teachers for North Africa, appeared to be emerging as a potential supplier of faculty for the needy and rapidly growing higher educational institutions of middle Africa, which will require 7,000 more teachers from other countries to help meet an expected rise in the student body from 46,000 in 1961 to 274,000 in 1981.

In addition to teachers, Egypt sends many religious emissaries abroad under al-Azhar's auspices. In 1962 alone, 854 religious emissaries were sent abroad, 384 to African countries, 260 of whom went to the Sudan.[32] One wonders whether the expansion in this field might be in part a substitute for the announced but unfulfilled plan to send "religious attachés" to U.A.R. embassies in Africa.

Still another group President Nāṣir is thought to have attempted to use was the Levantine mercantile community in West Africa. In June, 1960, the U.A.R. Government established an "Emigré Arab Citizenship Certificate" for all those Arabs living abroad who had lost their nationality. It also attempted to hold a Congress of Emigrés, and placed a Minister in charge of affairs dealing with Syrians and Lebanese living in Africa.[33] The already existing anti-Levantine feeling against Syrian and Lebanese traders in West Africa was bolstered by the apprehension of African leaders concerning the use Nāṣir might make of the Levantines in their countries. President Nkrumah of Ghana may have harbored such suspicions when Ghana became independent in 1957. It has been suggested that his warning at the All-African People's Conference in December, 1958, that "colonialism and imperialism may come to us yet in a different guise—not necessarily from Europe" may have been directed at least in part toward the U.A.R., which insisted on sending many more than its share of delegates to the conference.

President Nāṣir has also provided free headquarters and other assistance to the political parties of revolutionary African nationalists. One of his advisers on African affairs, 'Abd al-'Azīz Ishaq, is raising the children of the late Patrice Lumumba in his home. An African Association, founded in 1955, today houses the offices of African parties from eight countries not yet independent, and one from the Republic of South Africa. Others have had offices in Cairo until their countries attained independence.[34]

The message of Islam is thus spread through many channels. The Supreme Islamic Council of al-Azhar provides literature for Islamic centers in Africa and elsewhere. A new organization with broader educational and social objectives is the Islamic Congress, founded in 1954 by Egypt and eight other diverse Islamic countries—Afghanistan, Indonesia, Iran, Morocco, Pakistan, Saudi Arabia, Syria, and Yemen. The Egyptian section was established by the military government as an agency of the Presidency of the Republic in November, 1954, shortly after the Muslim Brotherhood was dissolved. The rulers of other Muslim countries feared that the army officers ruling Egypt might use the Congress for political action abroad.[35] However, one of these officers, who became Secretary-General of the Islamic Congress, Anwar al-Sadat, insists that the activities of the Congress are non-political in character. In an interview with Majid Khadduri in the spring of 1958, he said that the politics of Muslim states are so divergent that the idea of Muslim unity through the restoration of the caliphate had been abandoned. Pakistan, for example, allied itself with the West, while Egypt favored positive neutrality.

According to al-Sadat, his office was in contact with about 350 Muslim agencies and organizations representing 450 million Muslims throughout the world. The major problems of Islam, he said, were (1) that Muslims were divided between Sunnī and Shī'ī sects, (2) that some Muslims were still under colonial rule, (3) that many Muslims were Muslims only in name, and (4) that many Muslims are very backward economically and socially.

Al-Sadat took the position that there is no incompatibility between Islam and nationalism. "We want to stimulate the national consciousness in each country," he said, as the basis for the Islamic structure in that country. All Muslims, except those under colonialism, are urged to be loyal to their own rulers. Those who are free should help to free those who are not. The Arabs should unite, but on the basis of Arab nationalism, not religion. The Islamic Congress, he concluded, had no use for politicians who exploit religion for political purposes.[36]

V

In secular Africa, where politics is king and the religion is nationalism, we have seen that Islam is not a useful instrument of foreign policy. Where it is used, it is often confused with Pan-Arabism and Nasserism in an amalgam so vague in objective that it naturally arouses suspicions and discord. In the solid Islamic area of North Africa, President Nāṣir of the United Arab Republic and President Bourguiba of Tunisia have, in their diverse ways, attempted to use Islam to assist the process of modernization. However, the differences among the five heads of state in North Africa are too deep at present to be overcome by Pan-Islamism and Pan-Arabism combined. Whether the future will bring greater unity if modernization spreads throughout North Africa and new leaders take over, remains to be seen.

South of the Sahara, President Senghor in Senegal and several Muslim presidents have also sought to use Islam to some extent to assist the process of modernization. But Islam is seldom considered as a basis for national unity, partly because of the determined secularity of the leaders, partly because of the differences between progressives and conservatives, and partly because of the need for good relations among the mixed Christian, Muslim, and animist populations of the area. Politicians will no doubt use Islam from time to time in irredentist movements and in other ways, but such tactics are more likely to disrupt than to cement good relations among African states.

President Nāṣir now appears to realize that his tactics have backfired. Despite his constant efforts to obtain denunciations of Israeli imperialism and neocolonialism, we have seen that nine of the thirteen heads of state of the Afro-Malagasy Union have visited Israel. At the sixteenth and seventeenth sessions of the United Nations General Assembly, moreover, the U.A.R. suffered considerable discomfiture when a majority of these nine states, plus Liberia and Sierra Leone, sponsored resolutions calling for direct negotiations between the Arabs and Israelis. By the fall of 1962, Israel had established diplomatic relations with twenty-one African countries, had about 1,000 technicians in more than thirty-five African states and territories, and had about 1,000 African students in Israel.[37] Meanwhile, by May, 1963, embassies from sixteen African governments had been established in Cairo, and President Nāṣir appeared to be more circumspect in many of his African activities. At the Addis Ababa summit meeting on

May 24, 1963, while he stated that a group of African states "share our view that Israel is a tool of imperialist infiltration to Africa and one of its bases of aggression," he declared that in a spirit of unselfishness the United Arab Republic would forego raising the Israeli issue.[38]

In West Africa, we have noted that the Muslim brotherhoods and marabouts were shielded for a long period from the various reform movements of the Mediterranean world. The great majority of West Africa's conservative marabouts, in the view of Virginia Thompson and Richard Adloff, "are too venal and ignorant to comprehend the danger that threatens their long-held power over the Negro masses."[39] Possibly in the future, West Africa may witness internal struggles for power among the Islamic groups themselves, or between them and the secular modernizers, a development that could have a significant impact on foreign relations.

The nature of Islamic groups in West Africa is so complex, however, that generalizations are extremely hazardous. Thomas Hodgkin has demonstrated this in a careful delineation of (1) the kinds of Islamic institutions and ideas that tended to retard the development of nationalist movements, and (2) those that tended to assist the development of nationalist movements. He even finds that certain groups, the Tījānīyah for example, have different aspects which work in opposite directions. Hodgkin has opened up a wealth of research possibilities on Islam in West Africa.[40]

This chapter has dealt mainly with relations among African leaders and governments. Many questions involved in person-to-person relationships also need exploration. What do African graduates of al-Azhar actually do when they return home? And what effect does the pilgrimage have on the many thousands of Africans who make the trip each year? It is important in renewing the African's sense of Islamic solidarity and his pride in belonging to a world-wide religion. Yet Sir Ahmadu Bello, Premier of the Northern Region of

Nigeria, who has made the pilgrimage seven times, writes: "It is regrettable but unfortunately true that many unscrupulous people make illegal gains by fleecing the pilgrim and taking from him on various pretexts as much of his savings as they can." [41] Many African pilgrims, therefore, find that they have to work on the way home. The Gezira (Jazirah) cotton project in the Sudan, for example, has benefited from the labor of thousands of pilgrims.

And what effect do racial differences and the memory of the slave trade really have on relations between Africans and Arabs? Is there a real basis for the remark a well-known African politician from Chad is reported to have made to a Sudanese cousin: "Why do you Negro Africans want to ally yourself with the Arabs? The color of your skin will always be against you." [42] Or is this mostly fiction? And what about the slave trade and the "bitter memory" of it? At the Casablanca Conference in 1961, Jacques Baulin reports, a member of the Mali delegation demanded from the Foreign Minister of Libya the extradition of a Mali tribal chief who had made the pilgrimage to Mecca with all the people of his village. While in Saudi Arabia, it appears, the chief had sold all his villagers into slavery and taken refuge in Libya himself.[43] This makes entertaining reading for Western readers, but is either the vestige of the slave trade, or the memory of it, politically significant in Arab-African relations?

Finally, let us take note of Douglas Ashford's survey of the attitudes of ninety-three Moroccan party secretaries, who did not draw significant political distinctions between Islamic and Arab influences in their evaluation of national problems. If the same results were found to be widely recurring, he suggests, we ought "to exercise more caution in attributing political behavior" to either Islamic or Arab influences.[44]

NOTES

1. For background information, see the three books of J. S. Trimingham, *Islam in Ethiopia* (London, 1952), *Islam in the Sudan* (London, 1949), and *Islam in West Africa* (London, 1959). Thomas Hodgkin's articles in many issues of the journal *West Africa,* particularly in 1956 and 1957, are outstanding. See also his critique of Trimingham's latest work, *A History of Islam in West Africa* (London, 1962), in "Islam, History and Politics," *Journal of Modern African Studies,* Vol. 1 (March, 1963), pp. 91–98. Other useful works include Alphonse Gouilly, *L'Islam dans L'Afrique occidentale française* (Paris, 1952); J. N. D. Anderson, *Islamic Law in Africa* (London, 1954); and E. W. Bovill, *The Golden Trade of the Moors* (London, 1958). An interesting account by a French- and Arab-speaking journalist is Jacques Baulin, *The Arab Role in Africa* (Baltimore, 1962).

2. John V. Taylor, "Christianity in Africa," *Africa: A Handbook to the Continent,* ed. Colin Legum (New York, 1961), pp. 465–69.

3. "Amadou Hampaté Ba: A Propagator of the Moslem Faith," *Réalités,* September, 1960, pp. 48–50.

4. *Horoya* (Conakry), No. 47 (September 2, 1961), p. 1.

5. *Ibid.,* No. 45 (August 29, 1961), p. 1.

6. *West Africa,* December 22, 1962, p. 1411.

7. William Foltz, "The Political Parties of Senegal," to appear in the forthcoming *Political Groups in Middle Africa,* eds. James S. Coleman and Carl G. Rosberg, Jr.

8. *Paris International* broadcast, 2000 GMT, May 31, 1961-E.

9. *Paris International* broadcast, 2000 GMT, June 7, 1961-E.

10. Sir Ahmadu Bello, *My Life* (Cambridge, 1962), p. 192.

11. *Awo: The Autobiography of Chief Obafemi Awolowo* (Cambridge, 1960), p. 312.

12. *West Africa,* April 22, 1961, p. 445; *Africa Report,* April, 1961, p. 10.

13. William H. Lewis, "Islam and Nationalism in Africa," *The Arab Middle East and Muslim Africa,* ed. Tibor Kerekes (New York, 1961), pp. 72–73.

14. *West Africa,* April 6, 1963, p. 379.

15. Thomas Hodgkin, "Sectarianism in the Sudan," *West Africa,* October 27, 1956, p. 849.

16. Ghana Information Services (New York), *News Bulletin,* May 27, 1963, p. 4.

17. *Carrefour Africain* (Ouagadougou), May, 1962.

18. J. H. A. Watson, "Mauritania: Problems and Prospects," *Africa Report,* February, 1963, pp. 3–6.

19. Douglas E. Ashford, "The Irredentist Appeal in Morocco and Mauritania," *Western Political Quarterly,* Vol. 15 (December, 1962), pp. 641–51.

20. From *al-Moujahid,* in Baulin, *op. cit.,* p. 114.

21. Don Shannon, "Ben Bella Star Rises as Nasser's Challenger," *Washington Star,* May 12, 1963.

22. "Islam in Modern Tunisia" (speech made by President Bourguiba at the Institute of Islamic Studies of McGill University, May 2, 1961), *News from Tunisia,* Bulletin No. 56, June 13, 1961 (Press Department, Embassy of Tunisia, Washington, D. C.), pp. 2–3.

23. Majid Khadduri, *Modern Libya* (Baltimore, 1962), pp. 334–36.

24. Gamel Abdel Nasser, *Egypt's Liberation: The Philosophy of the Revolution* (Washington, D. C., 1955), pp. 109–10.

25. Information furnished by the United States Information Agency, November, 1962.

26. Dr. 'Abdu al-Huli, "Al-Azhar in Asia and Africa," *Ahram al-Iqtisadi* (Cairo) February 1, 1963. (Translation from Arabic.)

27. Quoted in Baulin, *op. cit.,* pp. 40–41.

28. Bayard Dodge, *Al-Azhar—A Millenium of Muslim Learning* (Washington, D. C., 1961), p. 162.

29. From the London *Observer,* as cited in the *Washington Post,* March 30, 1963.

30. Baulin, *op. cit.,* p. 31.

31. "An African Policy for Egypt," *Egyptian Economic and Political Review,* Vol. 2 (August, 1956), p. 22.

32. 'Abdu al-Huli, *op. cit.*

33. Baulin, *op. cit.,* p. 54.

34. *Washington Post,* May 18, 1963.

35. P. J. Vatakiotis, "Dilemmas of Political Leadership in the Arab Middle East: The Case of the United Arab Republic," *American Political Science Review,* Vol. 55 (March, 1961), pp. 103–4.

36. I am indebted to my colleague Majid Khadduri for this information from his notes on a conversation with Anwar al-Sadat in the spring of 1958.

37. Smith Hempstone, "Moslems Warned Israelis Threaten to Obliterate Islam in East Africa," *Washington Post,* September 25, 1962.

38. As quoted by Jay Walz, *New York Times,* May 25, 1963.

39. Virginia Thompson and Richard Adloff, *French West Africa* (Stanford, 1957), p. 578.

40. Thomas Hodgkin, "Islam and National Movements in West Africa," *Journal of African History,* Vol. 3 (1962), pp. 323–27.

41. Bello, *op. cit.,* p. 192.

42. Quoted in Virginia Thompson and Richard Adloff, *The Emerging States of French Equatorial Africa* (Stanford, 1960), p. 97.

43. Baulin, *op. cit.,* p. 41.

44. Douglas E. Ashford, "The Political Usage of 'Islam' and 'Arab Culture,'" *Public Opinion Quarterly,* Vol. 25 (Spring, 1961), p. 114.

APPENDIX

RELIGIOUS AFFILIATIONS IN AFRICAN COUNTRIES *

	Population Total [a]	*Catholics*	*Protestants*	*Muslims*	*Animists*
Algeria †	10,896,940	942,322	15,650	9,780,232	c
Angola	4,500,000	1,539,000	559,000	c	2,114,000
Basutoland	641,674	273,542	213,000	c	136,000
Bechuanaland	304,097	6,230	37,404	c	260,463
Burundi	2,495,000	1,600,000	100,000	20,000	775,000
Cameroon	3,873,548	776,972	b	605,379 d	b
Central African Republic	1,180,000	128,000	128,000	50,000	830,000
Chad	2,652,000	75,615	78,000	1,400,000	1,062,385
Congo (Brazzaville)	803,745	257,866	134,650	4,540	382,000
Congo (Léopoldville)	13,990,162	4,873,925	1,058,072	116,372	7,300,314
Dahomey	1,756,000	238,148	17,600	123,000	1,341,000
Egypt	26,000,000	42,000 RC 1,500,000 Copts	200,000	24,000,000	c
Ethiopia (+Eritrea)	17,000,000	124,000	b	b	b
Gabon	417,000	185,260	c	202,445	c
Gambia	280,500	4,451	3,500	214,000	58,000
Ghana	6,690,730	562,912	686,000	687,000	4,658,133
Guinea	2,727,000	25,110	1,000	1,700,000	1,000,000
Guinea, Portuguese	550,000	15,000	c	165,000	320,000
Guinea, Spanish	240,000	192,731	c	950	65,000
Ivory Coast	3,240,000	235,836	69,574	678,455	2,193,237
Kenya	6,668,417	766,792	370,000	580,000	3,773,000
Liberia	1,500,000	12,804	60,000	250,000	1,176,000
Libya	1,172,000	41,285	3,500	1,124,000	c
Malagasy Republic	5,186,331	1,085,741	859,159	252,205	2,953,922
Mali	3,745,875	18,607	1,962	2,331,150	1,383,399

* Source: *Ready Information About Africa* (Mission Information Center, St. Edward's College, London, 1962).

† Figures for Algerian Catholics and Protestants are in error due to large-scale exodus of Europeans since 1962.

[a] Differences between the population total and the sum of the categories are frequently accounted for by "Catechumans" not yet in the Catholic Church. Among other unlisted categories are Jews, Greek Orthodox, and Hindus.

[b] Not listed.

[c] None or few.

[d] Derived from *Ready Information About Africa* and *Africa Report,* Vol. 8 (March, 1963), p. 14.

	Population Total [a]	Catholics	Protestants	Muslims	Animists
Mauritania	730,000	2,678	c	721,000	c
Morocco	10,560,000	420,844	7,000	9,900,000	c
Mozambique	6,310,000	476,700	100,000	612,000	4,663,500
Niger	2,600,000	10,600	579	1,800,000	727,547
Nigeria	34,443,000	1,750,000	1,030,000	15,090,000	15,870,000
Northern Rhodesia	2,394,900	486,114	30,092	837	1,872,199
Nyasaland	2,800,000	444,734	500,000	209,000	1,582,000
Rwanda	2,572,773	654,813	138,939	13,413	1,499,125
Senegal	2,260,000	143,225	900	1,633,500	474,428
Sierra Leone	2,300,000	18,545	70,000	800,000	1,400,000
Somalia	2,500,000	3,880	c	2,200,000	c
Somaliland (Fr.)	75,024	4,280	120	70,000	c
South Africa	14,673,000	850,230	9,379,000	102,600	3,667,000
South West Africa	593,000	62,399	104,000	c	423,000
Southern Rhodesia	3,111,700	279,462	114,947	1,596	2,154,732
Spanish Sahara	24,550	4,860	c	19,600	c
Sudan	11,615,000	259,971	20,000	8,000,000	3,000,000
Swaziland	264,300	20,068	56,795	c	204,205
Tanganyika	9,994,000	1,547,149	739,000	2,033,000	4,918,451
Togo	1,116,000	205,226	42,557	57,807	780,000
Tunisia	3,965,000	100,000	c	3,840,000	c
Uganda	6,536,616	1,701,348	719,028	65,366	3,979,032
Upper Volta	3,884,000	131,343	9,274	995,500	2,698,000
Zanzibar	299,111	2,080	c	296,000	c

Pan-Islamism in the Modern World: Solidarity and Conflict Among Muslim Countries

By T. Cuyler Young

It was just about a century ago, in the reign of Sultan Abdūlaziz of Turkey, that Pan-Islamism became a conscious movement and force in the Muslim world. The focus of the movement was the Sultan, in his claim as the Caliph of Islam —a claim that had been put forward toward the end of the eighteenth century but was not really exploited until the time of Abdūlaziz and Abdūlhamid II, in the 1860's and

1870's, and then embodied in the Ottoman constitution promulgated in 1876.

From the beginning the movement was ambivalent, with negative and positive, defensive and offensive aspects. It aimed to threaten or at least embarrass European powers that ruled colonies with substantial Muslim communities as well as to forge a unity within the Ottoman Empire that might resist the inroads of further European penetration and arrest the internal forces of disintegration. Within that empire the Arabs were the most numerous and important of the non-Ottoman peoples and the natural media, historically and psychologically, to promote the solidarity of Islam by expanding and deepening the centrifugal concept of the Sultan-Caliph. So it was that Abdūlhamid II gathered around him men of Arab origin, mostly identified with orders of mystics, who became the protagonists of the movement and used the holy language of the Qur'ān as the vehicle of their propaganda.[1]

Contributing to this same drive toward Pan-Islamism was another movement of reformers, led by the famous and dynamic Jamāl al-Dīn al-Afghānī, which was similarly motivated, negatively and positively, especially in reaction and resistance to the ascendant European powers. Afghānī, with his associates and disciples, operated in a wider Islamic context than the Ottoman Empire and looked upon the Sultan as no divinely ordained caliph except insofar as he might in such capacity further the wider cause of Islamic unity, beyond the frontiers of the Ottoman state.[2]

Centering attention upon the glories and superiorities of Islamic civilization, rather than religion *per se*, Afghānī, though driving for Pan-Islamic unity, helped transmit to Muslims this dominating nineteenth-century concept of civilization, along with its necessary concomitant, the idea of progress. These together were destined to involve Muslims in cultural problems and dilemmas similar to those of Europe when political patterns of power changed and the Western world became convulsed in its twentieth-century internecine wars that inevitably became global in scope. Afghānī was convinced that the deeply rooted doctrine and concept of the *ummah* (community) was something superior in Muslim civilization as compared to European and could save the Islamic world from the atavistic forces generated in Europe and bound eventually to be unleashed and to wreak havoc on any apparent solidarity in European civilization. Hence, his dynamic drive, passionate and primarily political, was toward the restoration of the unity of this *ummah* for the political power and social progress that could and would result.

Yet the dynastic dreams of the Ottomans and their Sultan-Caliph, as well as the dynamic drive of the radical reformers toward a renewal of Islamic civilization, both fostering Pan-Islamism and the revival of the *ummah's* political power at the turn of the century, were to be broken and become quite discredited by the harsh realities of World War I. The Sultan-Caliph in 1914 called for *jihād* (holy war) under his leadership; but not only did the Muslims of French Africa, Asiatic Russia,[3] and British India fail to rise in support of the Caliph's *jihād* (himself in alliance with the Central Powers),[4] even the Arabs and other subject Muslims of the Ottoman Empire took to partnership with the infidel enemy and rose in revolt.[5] Within a decade the empire was dismembered and replaced by a laic Turkish republic, together with a group of Arab protectorates and mandates that began, in disillusioned frustration, to fight their long, hard way to political independence and nationhood.

Pan-Islamism, as a movement driving for political power in sufficient unity to match, if not indeed surpass, the imperialistic strength of Europe, was shattered. The Caliph, who as Sultan had primarily exploited the movement for national purposes of power, was hoist by his own petard and finished, and the frontal attack on the citadel of political power was routed. Moreover, Afghānī's reforming modernism, carried forward by that remarkable and influential al-Azhar teacher, Muḥammad 'Abduh, was likewise thwarted, though not destroyed. Insofar as the drive for political independence and power was concerned, the Arabs appeared no more successful than the Ottomans, continuing under the control of the victorious British and French. Certainly the drive for Pan-Islamic political power was shattered; but the arena of such struggle was only narrowed, and, though fragmented, entered a new phase of intensification in local nationalisms in which the drive for independence could be continued on many fronts. Forty years and another global war later, the nation-states of Islam are politically independent, all the way from Maghrib to Indonesia, although large communities of Muslims remain as minorities in states controlled by other communities.

The whole pattern and atmosphere of Pan-Islamic relations changed with the subsequent abolition of the caliphate and the establishment of a laic state in Turkey, together with the concomitant self-absorption of Arab nationalism. As for the Arabs, we may anticipate a later discussion [6] and point out that a thorough review by an ardent Muslim of different Arab nationalist theorists finds them all inadequate because they fail to give Islam a truly pre-eminent place in the dynamic concept and spirit of Arabism, although some of them, designated as "ambivalent," have a high appreciation of the role of Islam. Relevant also in this connection is the conclusion of Professor Leonard Binder regarding the relative position of the Arab nation and Islam as held by contemporary government leaders in Syria and Egypt: "Despite the variety of emphasis and expression in the writings of all these men, they all seem to be in general agreement. Aflaq [Ba'th theorist] and 'Abd al-Nāsir put nationalism above Islam and would have Islam serve nationalism. Neither excludes or opposes Islam." [7]

This is perhaps well illustrated in the more complex situation in India by the shifts in thinking and action on the part of Islamic leader Abu'l Kalām Āzād, who was an ardent Muslim nationalist until the early 1920's, but thereafter shifted to the role of nationalist Muslim, supporting Gandhi and the All-India Congress to the end and functioning until his death in 1958 as India's Minister of Education. He opposed the Pakistani separatist policies of Muḥammad Iqbāl and 'Alī Jinnāh, who, oddly enough, reacted oppositely: though they had earlier been strong nationalist Muslims, they took up the cause of Muslim nationalism and succeeded in splitting the subcontinent into two independent states.[8]

The reasons for these strange shifts following the failure of the Khilāfat movement in India are complex and rooted in the previous relationships of the Muslim and Hindu communities, especially vis-à-vis the British.[9] The irony of the subsequent development is deepened by the gradual convergence of the programs of these strong Muslim League nationalists and the Islamic fundamentalists in India, each in its different way romanticizing the ideal of early, original Islam. The result was the eventual emergence of Pakistan as a separate local nation, albeit with pretensions, ultimately to become illusions, of being an ideal Islamic state and society which might lead the Muslim world to new universalism and power.[10]

It is appropriate, therefore, to note here certain activities of Pakistan since partition, to which M. K. Nawaz calls attention. Arising out of this pretension to, and vague idea of, Pakistani leadership toward the ideal of a universal Islamic society, these activities, ironically, are really motivated by, and more concerned with, Pakistan's local political policies and programs than with any Pan-Islamic political power structure or problems. Soon after independence Pakistan tried to form such a grouping of Muslim nations, but did not even succeed in convening an intergovernmental conference. In 1954 there was held in Pakistan an International Economic Conference, but no successor or permanent structure developed. Again in December, 1957–January, 1958, Lahore was host to a second International Islamic Colloquium but no integrative results were achieved; indeed, the participant was more impressed by the rivalry of delegations, especially the Egyptian and Syrian, both trying to prevent Pakistan from securing any political advantage from the gathering. Political expediency compromised the cultural and scholarly aims of the originators of the first such colloquium, but it was that of rival nation-states, not any political purpose of Pan-Islamism.

Or, again, consider Pakistan's relations with the Arabs in the Suez crisis. Eight days before the invasion of Suez, the Foreign Minister of Pakistan is reported to have said: "Pak-Islamism and not Pan-Islamism should now be the slogan. You have no future if you indiscriminately fight or die for Moslems outside Pakistan even though they be the dearest friends of your enemy." [11] Although Pakistan did not side with the invader, it did not support Egypt in the same way as other Asian countries, for example, India and Indonesia; and later Egypt refused to accept Pakistan's contingent among the United Nations troops in the Gaza strip.

Professor Khadduri elsewhere [12] refers to the Muslim aspiration to form a bloc in the international community, presumably in the United Nations, designating this neo-Pan-Islamism. Yet this has never gone beyond the stage of pious aspiration; actualities are otherwise. Mr. Nawaz rightly notes that although there are varied blocs of nations—OAS, NATO, SEATO, Arab League, Communist bloc, neutralists, and others—to date there has yet to be formed anything approaching an Islamic bloc. On the issue of Israel there is the nearest approximation to it; but this is the individual specific, the exception that proves the rule. There is no Muslim bloc, nor are there indications that one is likely soon to emerge.

To summarize, and to conclude with an apt quotation,

Pan-Islamism today is little concerned with any immediate hope of unified or widespread political power or organization.

> It is only a few Muslims here and there who disagree with the modern consensus that the rehabilitation of Islam throughout the world is taking place and ought to take place in terms of local rehabilitation. The pan-Islamic vision today is essentially the envisaging of each of the Muslim nations or communities—Arab world, Turkey, Iran, Pakistan, Indonesia, etc.—individually regenerated, revitalized, prosperous, and strong. Such a vision adds to the particular nationalism of each region only the hope—or the presupposition—that these would all cooperate in friendly mutuality.[13]

Yet, according to Professor Sokol, in Soviet Russia Pan-Islamism apparently is still taken very seriously (at least it was as late as 1955),[14] since it is believed to have been used not only against the Soviets during the Civil War and by the Nazis in World War II, but also more recently by American and English imperialists "for the struggle against the national-liberation movement in the countries of the East." [15] Muslims were the last to lay down their arms in the struggle against the Bolshevik government; the Basmaji movement in Russian Central Asia was not finally squelched until 1933, when the third serious rising had taken place. Soviet concern with the loyalty of its 25 million Muslims is understandable when it is realized that in World War II they deserted to the Nazis in large numbers; from Turkestan alone there were 180,000 who served in the Wehrmacht or Waffen-SS.[16]

Muslims generally, however, though little concerned with Pan-Islamic political power, are thinking in terms of the religious and cultural rehabilitation of the total community.[17] Our immediate task is to assess some of the liabilities and assets of this widespread concern and experience.

II

Clearly, the core of any unity in Pan-Islamism is the common faith of Muslims. From Morocco to the Philippines this unity in faith has power amidst remarkable political, social, and cultural diversity; it is so even amidst the sectarian divisions built into the Islamic heritage by the faith itself, not to mention those arising from outside pressures.

The strength of this unity naturally depends upon communications and the interchange of experience in faith. Historically the pilgrimage in this respect has been a medium of intercourse and a bond of unity. It still so functions. Yet, for all its present comparative ease of accomplishment and spectacular increase in absolute numbers,[18] it is doubtful if, relatively, this institution is as important in the modern world as previously. Probably at no time was the younger generation of a period heavily represented, but one is inclined to estimate, in the absence of any statistics, that today there is a much smaller proportion of younger Muslims participating. Modern status seekers are not so likely to put the title of *Hajji* so high on their list of ambitions. Ambitious politicians may always be conspicuous exceptions to any such generalizations.[19]

The ease and increase of communications generally among Muslims, however, are of significance. The exigencies of internationalism, be it of diplomacy, trade, economic development, education, technology, and the like, are mixing men everywhere, except in the curtained societies; and the Muslim countries are not today to be counted among these, despite visa restrictions, which for the most part are economically motivated.

Increase in communications does not in itself inevitably mean better relations among peoples; often the opposite is true. Yet in the long run the increase in authentic information must lay a more solid base nearer reality for appreciation and understanding. The vast apparatus for mass communications, if responsibly used, should over time increase rather than diminish understanding, if for no other reason than that the realities of possible association are made clear.

Certainly this should be true of the vast Islamic world with its common faith, albeit diversely understood and practiced. There are signs that increased intercourse among Muslim countries and peoples is providing the basis for new self-understanding among Muslims. At the Princeton University–Library of Congress International Colloquium of Islamic scholars held a decade ago, it was significant how the Muslims present became aware of each other, most admitting that they knew more about the West, its history, civilization, thought, and relation to their own respective countries, than they did about each other, despite their common faith and culture, and in many instances, neighborly proximity.

This long and deep absorption of most Muslim countries with the dynamic and aggressive West, technologically and industrially so far ahead of them, is bound to continue for some time to come. Now that political independence has been achieved, the context and mood of this concern may be shifting, although in the atomic age the reality of such independence for all nations has been relatively attenuated; and this in itself disturbs the corporate *psyches* of emergent states and compounds the complexity of relations between the Islamic and Western worlds. There has been much of the cement of negativism holding diverse Muslim peoples and states together: the common struggle to attain political freedom from the dominating imperialism of the West. Much of this "negative cement" inevitably will continue to be manufactured, for there is still the major problem of Eastern economic dependence and Western domination to be solved; and as long as the technological and industrial gap between the Islamic states and those of the West obtains, absorption with the West and a negative reaction to its economic affluence and power will continue. On the other hand, there is evidence that newly won independence has altered the context and mood of concern enough to turn the attention of an increasing number of Muslims inward to a consideration of the truly constructive moves that must be made to cope with the forces of disintegration and to discover ways and means for readjusting the foundations on which true Muslim unity can be solidly built in the modern world.

A paramount question, of course, relates to the nature of the foundations on which any Islamic unity or solidarity is to be built. Searching for authentic self-knowledge and self-realization amid the strains and stresses of modern life, the corrosive acids and potent catalysts of rapid social change, Muslims are essentially in no different a predicament than are the heirs to other great and ancient ethnic religious traditions elsewhere in the modern world. Especially is this true in comparison to Jews and Christians, whose religious systems are also built on a conviction of revelation, authoritative and final, but whose historical development and cultural articulation differ considerably from those of Islam. In contrast to certain advantages of Christianity for adjustment to some of the demands of modernity are the disadvantages and the sudden, excessive shock experienced by Islam. It is no wonder that Islamic societies appear in such disarray and that Muslims are confused.

As in the West, so in the Muslim world there is an increase in secularism and secularists, many of them espousing materialistic philosophies of one kind or another; yet even so, because historically patriotism and cultural identity have been coterminous with the community of the faithful, many of these moderns resent any implication that they are not Muslims, though they reject the religious faith both in theory and practice. Although a minority, this group steadily increases; it is the vanguard in the creation of new dimensions in a pluralistic society. Such a group's contribution to Pan-Islamism is limited to the enhancement of the common cultural heritage. Although it may not initiate hostility to moves toward religious communal solidarity, this could be evoked by certain decisions and designs of more conservative traditionalists.[20]

In the development of the common faith in the future, it is altogether possible that the center of concern and focus of attention of the *'ulamā'* and the religious intellectuals may shift from the *Sharī'ah* and its relation to modern society to *kalam* (the word of God, later coming to mean scholastic theology), for such would seem to be the increasing demand of the modern thinker and activist. A theology reformed, or at least restated in terms to fit the need and the understanding of modern man, is imperative if there is to be developed any new and vital religious unity among Muslims. And concomitant with this, there will surely be new efforts in the field of philosophy, to forge on the anvil of revelation and *kalam,* under the hammer blows of reason, perhaps even heated to malleability by the bellows of a new mysticism, a more satisfying *Weltanschauung* that may present the essentials of the faith as succor and support, illumination and motivation for modern man as, in the "dark night of the soul," he copes with the "ambiguity of the human condition" and gropes his way to an experience of grace and peace.

Afghānī first, and then 'Abduh and his successors, laid out these lines of thought and action, followed and explored since by most modernizers of Islamic thought, when they centered attention upon the doctrines of revelation and divine transcendence, capable of confirmation and explication by reason, and all authenticated in vigorous obedience by submissive but activist man.

Much will depend upon what group and what point of view lead and dominate in the revival and reform of Islamic thought, especially theological and philosophical. Certainly there are extreme rightist elements and fundamentalists who will endeavor to hold the line of the heritage at every point and in every sector, such as the eclipsed Muslim Brotherhood among the Arabs, the Devotees of Islam among the Persians, the followers of Mawdūdī among the Pakistanis. Given again favorable circumstances, they may return to some influence, but it is unlikely that over any length of time, with the accelerated pace of modernization and the demands of development in every field connected therewith, there could be any serious bid by such groups for a determining role in shaping any new Islamic solidarity that is likely to have staying power.

But what of the substantial numbers of the traditionalists who are becoming increasingly aware of these problems but find it difficult to reduce substantially the area of the faith's dominance if not specific control and, at least in theory and ideal, insist upon its totalitarian rule? In the long run it is probably among these that the issues will be decided. They are at once the hope and despair of those striving from within, or looking from without, for Muslim solidarity and unity in a form compatible with the apparent demands of a modern pluralistic society.

Professors Gibb and Wilfred Smith have set forth and documented the proposition that any real and abiding reconstruction of Muslim thought as a basis for true unity of the *ummah* must come from the ranks of the orthodox *'ulamā'* and not from the modernists who have to date appeared. To quote the latter:

> It is profoundly true that the problems of the Muslim world cannot be adequately met unless men have an intellectual honesty, self-critical humility, and some kind of effective faith. Yet it is also true that they cannot be solved unless men are aware of what the problems are. Our study here would suggest that Gibb is right at least for the Arab world in stating that "the

future of Islam rests where it has rested in the past"—on the orthodox *'ulamā'*. But as he goes on to say, they have yet to come to grips with the modern world.[21]

Here lies the crux of the whole question: There has yet to be built that bridge between those of modern mind and action and those of tradition; as yet, there is not even any agreement as to where the pylons are to be placed, let alone agreement as to the nature of the connective roadway. The future of the *ummah* and any unity it may enjoy wait upon this work of social, intellectual, and spiritual engineering.

III

One would expect that in regard to culture there would be more agreement among Muslims everywhere and a nearer realization of cultural affinity and unity across the broad expanse of the Islamic world from the Atlantic to the Pacific. To a large degree, agreement manifests itself in various ways, perhaps most clearly in the affinities of Muslim members of the so-called Afro-Asian bloc of countries. Yet even here there are frictions and something less than unanimity, granted the remarkable achievements of Islamic unity amidst inherited cultural diversity. Moreover, beneath the surface, there appear cultural clashes between major sections of the Muslim world, and within some of these parts, serious divergences in regard to culture.

However much cultural differences in classical times were submerged in the universal civilization of the Islamic community, in which Arabic was the *lingua franca* of science and learning, theology and philosophy, and even much of literature until the renaissance of Persian, in the modern world there has developed distinctive cultural self-consciousness among Arabs, Berbers, Turks, Persians, Afghans, Indians and Pakistanis, and Indonesians. To be sure, this is tied to modern nationalism, but it is a mistake historically to think that this phenomenon of differentiation had not appeared centuries ago in the Islamic world; although it may be granted that the modern Western form of nationalism emphasizes substantially the common cultural heritage of the people trying to develop a modern nation-state. Such cultural differentiation is part of the postclassical period of Islamic history, so that for long, Ottoman, Persian, and Indian Muslims have been aware not only of a common Islamic cultural heritage but also of distinctive differentiations in accordance with a cultural heritage that reaches back to pre-Islamic time. This rich and hospitable soil accounts for much of the recent remarkably rapid growth of modern nationalism in the Islamic world.

Much of what is often indicated as political and nationalistic rivalry and friction among the various Muslim states—Arabs, Turks, Persians, and Pakistanis, for example—is really rooted more deeply in cultural diversity and is so to be understood. These people well know that Islam as conceived and practiced in these different areas by these different peoples is not uniform in nature though it may be distinctively unified in essential Islamic spirit. Yet even here there are distinctive differences, such as those between Sunnī Turks and Shīʿī Persians; and in the modern world, between laic Turks and orthodox Arabs. The Islam of northern India may have taken much of its distinctive form from the Persian culture through which most of it passed historically, but there are still further indigenous developments of it that are due to the cultural substructure of the subcontinent. Hence there are cultural differences, though less than in most relationships, between Persians and Pakistanis.

To illuminate this problem, I would call attention to two different approaches to Arab culture: The first is that enunciated just before World War II by an Arab intellectual, Costi Zurayk, whose discussion of Arab culture and nationalism has been very influential,[22] and whose little book, published after the defeat of the Arabs by the Israelis, entitled *The Meaning of the Disaster,*[23] was widely read and pondered by Arabs; the second is that to be found in I. R. A. al-Furuqi's *On Arabism: 'Urūbah and Religion.*[24] Together they point up a profound crisis in Arab culture in relation to the modern world.

Professor Zurayk, speaking of the "Essence of Arab Civilization," [25] emphasizes the attitudes of Arab civilization—"the spiritual urge, the universal outlook, the deep-seated belief in the unity of truth. . . . [and] most remarkable and distinctive . . . the cooperative nature of Arab culture." "Arab civilization is not the achievement of one people: it is rather a cooperative enterprise taken by many peoples of various racial origins, cultural backgrounds, and religious affiliations. Moslems, Christians, and Jews; Arabs, Arameans, Persians, Turks, Berbers, and others—all shared together in this common effort." In answer to the question of what the Arabs themselves contributed to the whole process, he says:

> Leaving aside the distinctive contributions of the Arabs—the original spiritual revival, the genius of the language, the faculty of expressing condensed experience in sharp clear-cut verse or prose, the individual achievements of Arabs in the various disciplines—leaving aside all this, I wish to venture the suggestion that even if the Arabs had themselves offered no single element to this whole, it is sufficient to their undying credit that they provided the original spirit and the necessary conditions for the bringing together and the cooperation of all these various peoples in one common effort. It was they who started the empire on a policy of tolerance, who opened their gates in Damascus, Baghdad, Cordova, and elsewhere to scholars of all races and sects, who sought scholars and books from the ends of the earth, who gloried in the patronage of the arts and the sciences. This alone is the most distinct contribution, more important than any single achievement in science or philosophy or art, and

entitles the Arabs to a marked place in the history of civilization.[26]

It is significant that Professor Zurayk, writing as a Christian Arab with profound pride in his people's past and in their contribution to human culture, underlines the universalistic outlook and cooperative attitude of classical Arab civilization, while at the same time paying tribute to the spiritual faith and belief in the unity of truth that animated the early generations of Arabs. These are characteristics of the early civilization which he admires and would like to see reinvigorated and enthroned in the modern Arab culture that is struggling toward unity and new self-consciousness. In such a broad and tolerant atmosphere there is room for the security and contribution of all pluralistic groups, whether they be of different religious faiths or of no faith at all. In such an atmosphere modern man, be he of the majority or of the minority, may thrive in serenity and peace. Needless to say, there are substantial numbers of modern Arabs who believe in this kind of Arab cultural unity, and hope and work for its realization, convinced as is Zurayk that it is their prideful heritage from the past and their only viable program for the future.

There are, however, quite different, if not indeed contradictory concepts of valid Arab culture, both in the past and the present. Conceived and developed by Muslims, these ideas of culture are concerned primarily with the communal majority of Arab society and its assimilation of culture to Islamic beliefs and ends. As an illustration of one such philosophy of culture, I would call attention to al-Furuqi's recent discussion of Arabism and religion, one of the boldest and most comprehensive known to me, and for that very reason very useful in this context.

This is a bold innovation in the field primarily because it shifts the totalitarian claims usually associated with Islamism to Arabism; or perhaps, more accurately, it appears so to make the shift, for clearly such extension of Arabism in depth and breadth is stimulated by the implications of the Islamic conviction that Muḥammad is the Seal of the Prophets and God's revelation through him final, all-embracing, and wholly determinant for man, particularly for his society and its organization. It is startlingly comprehensive, both in depth and breadth, because it elaborates the proposition that

> the Arab stream of being (of which *'urūbah* is the soul) is infinite like time. Neither its beginning nor its end can become an object of knowledge. It has always existed, though the consciousness of its existence may have started to be at a certain time. But even this consciousness is as old as history, although it has known periods of comparative weakness and strength. The *locus classicus* of this stream of being is the Arabian Peninsula, "the fount of pure Semitism" and the principal source of the stream.[27]

To equate Arabism with what most historians of culture would designate as Semitism is bold indeed, but here al-Furuqi does not stop; he goes on to assimilate into Arabism all those areas and cultures where the Semitic influence has predominated, including, of course, all those under Islamic dominance at any time. Reviewing the flow of this stream to engulf the Fertile Crescent, then North Africa, the savannah lands south of the Sahara, most of the Nile Valley and East Africa, all of Western Asia, the Russian steppes, and the Danube basin, he goes on to state:

> All the peoples inhabiting these lands are Arabs inasmuch as they partake of the Arab spirit which is the soul of the Arab stream of being. To do so is to recognize the Islamic valuational hierarchy, and to lay oneself open to determination by its member-values in their respective order of rank. The consensus (*ijmā'*) of the people may be the constitutive recognition of,

> and determinableness by, the value hierarchy. Doubtless, the clarity of understanding and, hence, the profundity of conviction on the one hand, and the forcefulness of determination on the other, differ as widely among individuals as nature's endowment of personal gifts to them. A Pakistani, a Nigerian or a Croatian may possess it in a degree as high as or higher than any Meccan, Syrian or Egyptian. But the commitment to value of the many communities within the stream on the whole varies in one direction only: It becomes progressively weaker, just as the stream water becomes progressively shallower, the further it is removed from the principal bed of the stream. . . .
>
> None of [these lands] has succeeded in extricating itself—except on the external and superficial level—of their Arab identity; and certainly none of them has found or created a non-Arab spirit by which they may identify themselves. The modern nationalist Turk, Persian, Indonesian or Nigerian may call himself non-Arab, but his consciousness still has no categories other than the Arab which it may call its own. His nationalism, whether deliberate or forced, old or new, is nothing but a naive provincialism which, however substantial, strong and energizing it may be, is still devoid of the sense of mission which gives a stream of being genuine significance. . . . As caricatures of their Western European archetypes, these nationalisms are doomed never to behold the universally moral, the ethically final, but to wallow in particularism and utility until a stream of being endowed with destiny and conscious of its mission—be it the Arab or some other stream—sweeps them off to oblivion.[28]

Certainly the Turks and Persians, Indonesians and Nigerians—even many of the pious Muslims among them—are not likely to take kindly to this Arab claim, sure to be regarded as cultured aggression. At least the Persians, I am fairly sure, will bristle with stunned affront and react with vigorous rejection. I can think of nothing better calculated, if widely comprehended in Iran, to revive the strong emphasis on pre-Islamic and ancient Persian culture that was so characteristic of Iranian nationalism in the interwar period of Rizā Shah. Islamic solidarity is scarcely furthered on the Anatolian and Iranian plateaus, or even on the plains of South Asia and the equatorial savannahs, by this kind of cultural aggrandizement: men there may be self-confessed and self-conscious Muslims, but Arabs they are sure they are not.

Nor are the minorities in Muslim countries, especially the Jews and Christians, even among the Arabs, to be attracted by al-Furuqi's Arab conquest of all ancient Semitism, including the Judaic and Christian attainments of universal monotheism and ethicality. Regarded by al-Furuqi as the first and second stages of Arab consciousness, and only preparatory to the climax of that consciousness in the reception by the Arabs of God's final revelation in the Qur'ān and by the Prophet Muḥammad, this whole process is complete and fulfilled when the *ummah* becomes the society of the Real, progressively approximating heaven's ideal unveiled by the Prophet in the Islamic value system. On the way, to be logical and consistent, al-Furuqi finds Hebrew separatism condemned and superseded by the higher monotheism of Judaism; and thereby he brands contemporary Zionism as inimical to God's chosen instrument of Arabism and excludes it from the realm of abiding truth and reality. Moreover, he finds Western Christianity, founded upon Pauline and Johannine thought, to be a usurper and perverter of the Arab triumph in the ethical and dynamic universalism of Jesus which establishes the abiding dignity and worth of the individual man; and thereby he places Western Christianity beyond the pale, exacerbates the recently mitigated division between Western and Eastern Christianity, and brands the West as the enemy of the truth in Arabism, as the imperialist oppressor of the Arab peoples, though now at last happily in withdrawal before the revival of *'urūbah* (Arabism).[29]

Taking his text from a dictum of Professor Gibb that to hold the mission of Muḥammad and the memory of the Arab

Empire as the central fact of all history is the essence of Arabness, Dr. al-Furuqi pays his disrespects to most of the intellectual champions of modern Arab nationalism and fences them about with critical strictures—whatever variety they may be: the "convinced" nationalists, N. A. Faris and M. T. Husayn, who, far from justifying their rejection of Gibb's proposition have "given us no valid substitute," have "not affirmed anything," but have "simply denied"; [30] the "confused" nationalists, 'Abd al-Rāzik and Khālid Muḥammad Khālid; and the "ambivalent" nationalists, Munif al-Razzaz, Hazim Nuseibeh, and Fayez Sayegh.

Of all the contemporary intellectuals discussing these subjects, al-Furuqi appears most appreciative of and nearest to agreement with Zurayk, whose *al-Wa'i al-qawmi,* and UNESCO address in Beirut in 1949, published in the *Middle East Journal,* referred to above, he discusses at some length. But even Zurayk fails: "Apart from resting on a one-sided interpretation of Arab culture and history," says al-Furuqi, "this view is obviously that of a sinking soul which can no more justify itself in its own eyes." [31] He lacks, for al-Furuqi, the courage of true *'urūbah* convictions. Zurayk sees too much good and validity in the West, believing that it must, for all its errors and excesses, be appreciated and learned from in many respects; and he affirms that Arabism must avoid excesses and endeavor to maintain a golden mean in which the virtues of both are achieved in harmony and unity. To such ironic sentiments and eclectic or synthetic procedures al-Furuqi is unalterably opposed. With Zurayk's emphasis upon Arabism's devotion to the "unity of truth" he is in accord, but he objects that "this unity of truth Zurayk conceived as discursive, not valuational. . . . The essence of Arab civilization must then be sought not in the discursive unity of truth, but in the axiological unity of human willing which accepted the truth as truth. Contrary to Zurayk's assertion, Arabic thought is not 'like that of the Latins, . . . one of reconciliation and synthesis' by nature, but by choice and decision, once the valuational fifth sense has been laid open to determination by the over-arching unity of God."

Furuqi concludes:

> This must have been the greatest creative act of the Arab spirit. It is immaterial that Arab civilization has used Hellenic, Persian, or Indian elements in the rubric of culture and civilization. No culture and no civilization can be free of elements borrowed from the outside. . . . The provision of an atmosphere of tolerance and such other conditions as may be necessary for collection and synthesis may be "sufficient to their (the Arab's) dying [*sic*] credit"; but it does not establish creativity, which remains a matter affecting the kind, rather than the mere existence of a synthesizing principle.[32]

One may surmise that Professor Zurayk will find these critical strictures too extensive and exclusive, too rigid and self-containing for acceptance, and the alternative Arabism set forth as too far out of touch with the modern world to be helpful in alleviating the world's pain and travail as it endeavors to move into some new era of acculturation and mutuality, the nature and the challenge of which far outrun the imagination as well as the accomplishments of the ancestors of classical times, whatever that time may be to which a people may look as the classical expression of their culture. The attempt to take a stance above and beyond the contemporary, to gain the perspectives of long history and eternal values, and hence not get ensnared in the confusions of the ephemeral and the partialities of the temporal, is laudable indeed and one may welcome such a vigorous presentation of a new and comprehensive approach to understanding one of the world's great and significant cultures. It should prove provocative and stimulative of new attempts at wrestling with some basic and axiomatic problems of human life, if it does not by its very vigor and forthrightness repel many within and without the Arab world—as more normally conceived—or suffer indifference from the many in both East and West who will conclude that it has not truly perceived nor come to grips with the creative and constructive elements in modern scientific and philosophical thought and in modern political and social action.

Whatever the result, the work certainly lays bare in a new and striking fashion many of the basic issues which now confront, confuse, and even convulse the contemporary Islamic world—issues which have by no means been settled in certainty or clarity in the modern West.

IV

Earlier, almost at the beginning of this paper, we stated that Pan-Islamism today is little concerned with any immediate hope of unified or widespread political power or organization, but is concerned rather with the other elements involved in Afghānī's dominating concept of civilization: the religious and the cultural. This we believe to be true as long as there is emphasis upon the "*immediate* hope." Not many Muslims and fewer outside observers would venture to believe that for the next generation or so there is much hope of any all-embracing Muslim political power that would integrate such distant and dissimilar states as Afghanistan and Algeria, Iran and Indonesia, Morocco and Malaysia, Pakistan and Nigeria. There are, however, those among the unreconstructed traditionalists who resist abandoning their dreams of this eventually being realized, though it be in the distant future. But what is of more immediate moment in all this discussion of Pan-Islamism, in the political sphere, is the conviction of the great majority of the traditionalists and the *'ulamā'* that Islam must continue to function as a state and that political organizations and institutions must be brought under the guidance and control of the Islamic leadership. Among the separate nation-states emergent throughout the Islamic world, they argue, this fundamental principle of essential Islamism must be made operative; only so can these countries be truly Islamic and can there be any hope whatever, even in the distant future, of creating a unified Islamic body of large power.

All along the line, as nations have emerged to independence, conservatives have fought for establishing the principle of Islam as the declared religion of the state, with this declaration inserted in the new constitutions adopted. For years Pakistanis tried to spell this out in detailed articles of the constitution they could not agree upon, and finally had to settle simply for the statement that Pakistan is to be known as an Islamic republic. To support this, recourse has been had to the democratic principle of the rule of the majority, which therefore means that in all these countries, except Lebanon, the state religion must be Islam. Shaykh al-Sibā'i of Syria so appeals and goes on to argue that Arab nationalism can eventually triumph only when Arab unity is achieved and that this can be successfully attained only by appealing to the great majority of Muslims, making sure that the states formed, and eventually federalized or unified, be officially Islamic.[33] The whole impact of the modern West, with which the Islamic world knows it has more affinity than with Asia farther east, despite all its resistance to imperialism and rejection of so much from the West, operates to weaken this theory in practice, aiding and abetting the development of those tendencies toward secularism which have been present in Islamic society for centuries. Moreover, the majority of the Muslim leaders in positions of power readily enough admire, adopt, and, once they have adopted, defend and expand many of those social changes that move in this direction: the reduction of the influence of the *Sharī'ah,* the new modern education, the emancipation of women, and the modification of authoritarian rule in favor of new democratic institutions.

Dr. Muḥammad al-Bahī of al-Azhar in a discussion of Islamic thought devotes a whole chapter to this problem of Islam as a state.[34] Rejecting Western criticisms of Islam for its political doctrines as based erroneously on the West's mistaken criteria for judgment, Dr. al-Bahī carefully develops the validity of the orthodox Islamic political theory on the basis of numerous Qur'ānic passages, affirming that only so can the personality of the Islamic community function in obedience to God and in fulfillment of its duty in the world under God, only so can independence be maintained and attacks resisted and the community make its devotion to the establishment of peace effective. Particularly is Islam charged with resisting unbelief and atheism, a task which can be effectively accomplished by the state devoted to Islamic goals and ends. This means in the contemporary world, above all, resistance to atheistic Marxism. Such resistance may arouse and galvanize Islam into new life and power, very much as did Islamic response to the Crusades from Europe, which in the more modern and recent form of imperialism has been successfully resisted by Islamic countries. The goals of the Islamic state are to preach and establish peace in the world, repulse all aggression (though such resistance must not itself become aggression), and make no truce with atheism; only a state that is truly and openly Islamic can hope to attain such goals. The Qur'ān clearly teaches that Islam is to be concerned not only with the proclamation of the message but also with the supervision of the machinery that implements that message in society among Muslims and between the Muslim and non-Muslim communities.

One might continue to document the proposition that the conservatives and traditionalists refuse to yield on this principle that Islam is a political power, a state. Even the modernizers, the Westernizers, are uneasy about this and feel that this principle is embedded in the Islamic revelation and the social philosophy as first practiced by the Prophet and his caliphal successors, at least the orthodox. The question at issue, of course, is what content and substance, what institutional form this Islamic principle demands. And here at once there appears a wide diversity of opinion and program.

This is a continuing source of friction among Muslims, ranging all the way from the modernizers to those conservatives and traditionalists who not only enunciate the principle but also continuously insist upon its implementation at all the levels of government. Some of the former are prepared to meet the theoretical challenge head on and reject the doctrine as inappropriate, if not impossible, in the modern world; while others, of a more political and pragmatic turn of mind, are prepared either to give the doctrine lip service or to dodge it, all the time resisting any effective implementation of it in matters of determining moment in the fashioning and functioning of political and social institutions. This, however, makes for a habit of indirection, if not deception, issuing in a certain insecurity, if not mistrust, in the society. This is a problem in every changing society, but more so in some than in others; an overdose of it can be unhealthy.

The remarks of Professor von Grunebaum in regard to this problem as it affects nationalism are also appropriate here, and they are sufficiently perceptive and thought-provoking to serve as a conclusion to this whole matter.

> Where does all this leave Near Eastern, Arab, Muslim nationalism? It will doubtless be compelled to continue Westernization; its self-realization, not to say its self-preservation, depends on increased admission of Western ideas and techniques—organizational, economic, cultural. At the same time conservative pressure will force the concealment of the borrowing, whenever

possible, behind the veil of the orthogenetic legend. Political stability, the most urgent short-range problem, is contingent upon the stabilization of self-respect, and self-esteem in turn depends on an amalgamation of prides: pride in the Muslim past and its assimilative powers, pride in the moral and intellectual courage to undertake an all but complete rebuilding of one's life structure and to embark on the most hazardous adventure open to man, the rethinking and redefining of his universe in range and kind, and of his own identity in it.[35]

NOTES

1. A. H. Hourani, *Arabic Thought in the Liberal Age, 1798–1939* (London, 1962), pp. 106 f. Professor E. D. Sokol, for whose comments on this paper I am pleased to express appreciation, calls my attention to Bernard Lewis, *The Emergence of Modern Turkey* (London, 1961), p. 336, n. 31, and p. 402, where it is indicated, on the basis of Christiaan Snouck Hurgronje, *Verspreide Geschriften*, Vol. 3 (Bonn, 1923), pp. 189 ff., that the role of the dervishes and brotherhoods in the Pan-Islamic movement has been exaggerated. This is probably true, but does not invalidate the restrained conclusions of Hourani, likewise based on the work of Hurgronje and on relevant Arabic sources (*op. cit.*, p. 107, n. 5).

2. Hourani, *op. cit.*, p. 108: "It would be truer perhaps to speak of a person than a movement, for this revolutionary pan-Islamism, this flood of religious feeling, national feeling, and European radicalism was embodied in the strange personality of a man whose life touched and deeply affected the whole Islamic world in the last quarter of the nineteenth century." For sources on his life, see *ibid.*, p. 108, n. 7; and for his less-known activities in India, the unpublished McGill University master's thesis of Sharīf Mujāhid, entitled *Sayyid Jamāl al-Dīn al-Afghānī* (Montreal, 1954).

3. Cf. E. D. Sokol, *The Revolt of 1916 in Russian Central Asia* (Baltimore, 1954), where the publicized risings in Russia are proved to have been provoked by the Czar's conscription of Muslims into army labor battalions.

4. In such an alliance he convinced no one that this was true *jihād*, or expansion of Islam. For this as the meaning of *jihād* and for a good brief discussion of the subject, see M. K. Nawaz, "The Doctrine of '*Jihad*' in Islamic Legal Theory and Practice," *Indian Yearbook of International Affairs*, Vol. 8 (1959), pp. 32–48; see also Professor Majid Khadduri's essay, pp. 24–39. Naturally the modern illustrations of Mr. Nawaz are mostly from Indian history. As one of the commentators on this paper, the author wishes to acknowledge not only this

reference but also with appreciation several points made by him and incorporated in the paper's final form.

5. Professor Sokol rightly observes that after 1908 the Young Turks were already more interested in Pan-Turkism than in Pan-Islamism, while the Arabs had similarly earlier taken to Pan-Arabism; see C. W. Hostler, *Turkism and the Soviets* (London and New York, 1957), p. 96, and Constantine K. Zurayk, "The National and International Politics of the Arab States," *Near Eastern Culture and Society*, ed. T. Cuyler Young (Princeton, 1951), p. 207.

6. See pp. 212–15 in this volume.

7. "Radical Reform Nationalism in Syria and Egypt," *Muslim World*, Vol. 49 (April, 1959), p. 110.

8. Hafeez Malik, "Abu'l Kalām Āzād's Theory of Nationalism," *Muslim World*, Vol. 53 (January, 1963), pp. 33–40.

9. See Leonard Binder, "Pakistan and Modern Islamic Nationalist Theory," *Middle East Journal*, Vol. 11 (1957), Part I, pp. 382–96.

10. *Ibid.*, Vol. 12 (1958), Part II, pp. 45–56. The support of the fundamentalists, essentially negative before independence in struggling against the British and the Congress, came later to be a thorn in the side of the leadership of the new state and to move more toward the critical and antinationalist position of the traditional *'ulamā'*.

11. *Asian Recorder*, Vol. 1 (1956), p. 1116.

12. See Professor Khadduri's essay in this volume, p. 36.

13. Wilfred C. Smith, *Islam in Modern History* (Princeton, 1957), p. 82. The quotation was used by Professor Sokol in his comments.

14. The date of the article on Pan-Islam in the *Bolshaya Sovetskaya Entsiklopedia*, 2d ed., Vol. 32, pp. 1–2.

15. *Idem.*

16. Olaf Caroe, *Soviet Empire: The Turks of Central Asia and Stalinism* (London, 1953), p. 247.

17. G. E. von Grunebaum, *Modern Islam: The Search for Cultural Identity* (Berkeley and Los Angeles, 1962), p. 205.

18. Approximately 400,000 in 1951, the total rose to 750,000 in 1961, and to more than a million in 1963; see *New York Times*, August 8, 1961, and May 19, 1963.

19. For example, compare Naguib (Najib) and 'Abd al-Nāṣir in their differing attitudes toward the *hajj:* "Naguib records that his second Hajj meant the renewal of his faith in the brotherhood of man. 'Abd al-Nāsir records the more jarring opinion that the only *raison d'être* of the Hajj is to serve as an Islamic world parliament which 'should become an institution of great political power' " (Binder, *Muslim World*, Vol. 49 [April, 1959], p. 110). As Binder points out, it is significant that Nāṣir in discussing the three spheres within which Egypt operates "refers last of all (after the Arab and African spheres) to an Islamic sphere."

20. Among these could be pressures to restore the traditional domain and influence of the *Sharī'ah;* but this is such a complex subject that, although not unrelated to this general subject, adequate discussion here would lead us too far afield.

21. Smith, *op. cit.*, p. 152. See H. A. R. Gibb, *Modern Trends in Islam* (Chicago, 1947).

22. *Al-Wa'i al-qawmi* (*National Consciousness*) (Beirut, 1940).

23. Originally published in 1948, translated by R. Bayly Winder (Beirut, 1956).

24. (Amsterdam, 1962.) Although this is not a work of scholarship, it is a serious treatise questing for some viable ideology whereby to define and to justify *'urūbah* as a way of life and system of values worthy of a man's commitment. Even those who may initially react to it as fantastic may well take it seriously as the expression of a certain point of view and serious attempt to construct a philosophy for modern Arabs, and watch carefully its reception by them.

25. *Middle East Journal,* Vol. 3 (April, 1949), pp. 125–29.

26. *Ibid.,* pp. 130–32.

27. al-Furuqi, *op. cit.,* p. 198.

28. *Ibid.,* p. 199.

29. *Ibid.,* chs. 2 and 3.

30. *Ibid.,* p. 125.

31. *Ibid.,* p. 142.

32. *Ibid.,* p. 144.

33. "The Establishment of Islam as the State Religion of Syria," translated by R. Bayly Winder, *Muslim World,* Vol. 44 (1954), pp. 217–26. Winder notes that the constitution adopted fell short of this step, only declaring that the president of the republic must be a Muslim and that Islamic law (*fiqh*) is the principal source of legislation (*ibid.,* p. 216).

34. *Al-Fikr al-islāmi al-ḥadīth wa-silatuhu bi-al-isti'mār al-gharbi* (*Modern Islamic Thought and Its Relation to Western Imperialism*) (3d ed.; Cairo, 1962). I am indebted to Dr. Butrous 'Abd al-Malik for this reference.

35. Grunebaum, *op. cit.,* p. 218.